T0274148

PRAISE FOR *A SMALL, STUBBORN TOWN*

'Extraordinary; filled with a deep sense of enduring humanity. Immensely powerful, timely and real'

— Philippe Sands, author of *East West Street*

'It would be wonderful if the story told in this beautiful little book were the author's invention. But alas, the story itself is pure truth. Andrew Harding's characters invite the reader into their daily struggle which we witness with awe and empathy. We are touched by their courage and dignity – qualities that the author must surely have possessed in equal measure to record these extraordinary events'

— Andrey Kurkov

'A short, brilliant book... Its characters could have walked out of a novel'

— *Financial Times*

'Riveting and vividly written ... this gripping story is the literary equivalent of a superb miniature painting'

— *The Observer*

'A short, brilliant book on the battle for Voznesensk. Harding captures the mixture of courage, bewilderment and mania of Ukrainians who decide to fight the invasion'

— Gideon Rachman, *Financial Times*

'Harding has told a mesmerising story of how in the face of a mighty army, ordinary people can sometimes turn and simply say, "No."'

— Sinclair McKay, *Mail on Sunday*

'Elegantly told ... a deceptively simple narrative that explains a great deal about the dynamics of this war and many others'

– Roger Boyes, *The Times*

'Harding recreates the fighting blow by-blow ... [and] the personalities of his interviewees come to life'

– *The Telegraph*

'A cracking story ... that never loses sight of the "murderous absurdity" of Russia's war'

– Justin Marozzi, *The Spectator*

'[A] remarkable story ... propulsive'

– *The Irish Times*

'This gripping account is the Russian invasion of Ukraine in microcosm'

– Lindsey Hilsum

'A piercing book: the story of extraordinary heroism by ordinary people, and an accessible, limpid account of what battle is actually like'

– James Meek

'Fascinating, vivid, often harrowing, and deeply moving. A must-read for anyone trying to grasp both the human dimension and larger dynamics of this brutal contemporary war'

– Fiona Hill, author of *There Is Nothing for You Here*

'A captivating tale of one Ukrainian town and a heartening story of people's defiance, ingenuity and spirit. Originally reported and beautifully written'

– Arkady Ostrovsky, author of *The Invention of Russia*

'Reads like a daring tale from WW2'

– Will Brown, *Tortoise Media*

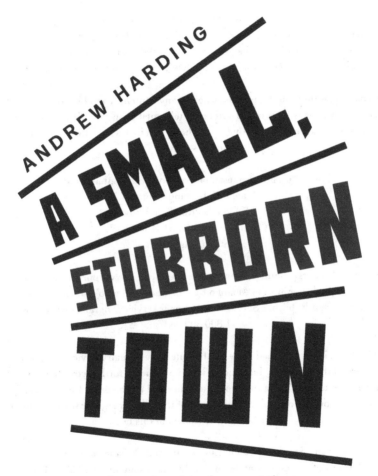

ANDREW HARDING

A SMALL, STUBBORN TOWN

Life, Death and Defiance in Ukraine

mango
PUBLISHING GROUP ™

Layout Design: Alex Kirby
Mango is an active supporter of authors' rights to free speech and artistic
expression in their books. The purpose of copyright is to encourage authors to
produce exceptional works that enrich our culture and our open society.

For permission requests, please contact the publisher at:
Mango Publishing Group
2850 S Douglas Road, 2nd Floor
Coral Gables, FL 33134 USA
info@mango.bz

For special orders, quantity sales, course adoptions and corporate sales, please
email the publisher at sales@mango.bz. For trade and wholesale sales, please
contact Ingram Publisher Services at customer.service@ingramcontent.com or
+1.800.509.4887.

This book is not intended to be a substitute for veterinary advice. If you are
concerned that your dog has a behavioural or other disorder, you should seek
veterinary advice. The author and publisher will not be liable for any loss or
damage in connection with or arising out of the performance or use of methods
described and contained in this book

A Small, Stubborn Town: Life, Death and Defiance in Ukraine
Library of Congress Cataloging-in-Publication number: 2023951102
ISBN: (pb) 978-1-68481-518-0 (e) 978-1-68481-519-7
BISAC: HISTORY / Europe / Ukraine HIS067000

The world will never be the way it was before.
We'll never let it
be the way it was before.

Serhii Zhadan, 'Rhinoceros',
Words for War: New Poems from Ukraine

To the people of Voznesensk

A Small, Stubborn Town: The People

Svetlana. A resident of Rakove village.
Misha. Svetlana's son, who collects scrap metal.
Petya. Svetlana's husband.
Valeri and Olya. Svetlana's brother and sister.

Yevhenii. The mayor of Voznesensk.
Andrii. The mayor's deputy.
Spartak. Head of the town council.

Roma, Slavik and Sasha. Friends of Misha's, who work on the town rubbish dump.
'Ghost'. Volunteer soldier and reconnaissance expert.
Valentyn and Zhenia. Local men who joined Voznesensk's home guard.

Igor. An officer in Russia's 126th Coastal Defence Brigade.
'Formosa'. Commander of the 2nd Battalion of Ukraine's 80th Airborne Assault Brigade.

Serhii. A Voznesensk resident.
Anna. Serhii's mother.

Alexander. A Voznesensk shopkeeper and volunteer home guard.
Mikhail. An ethnic Russian pensioner, living in Rakove village.
Mykhailo. A funeral director in Voznesensk.
Alexei. A Russian prisoner of war.

Dmytro. A major general in command of Ukrainian forces in Mykolaiv.
Vitalii. The Governor of Mykolaiv Province.

1.

'I'm going to count to three,' says the soldier.

Svetlana Martsynkovska meets his gaze with her small, bright, grey-green eyes. Just a kid, standing in her courtyard in his army uniform, pointing a gun at her soft, 59-year-old stomach.

'Good God,' she sighs.

Svetlana glances over at Zhulik, the angrier of her two dogs, who is snarling on his back legs and pulling against his chain. Her thumb moves, instinctively, to stroke the calluses on her right hand.

Svetlana is inclined to argue with the soldiers. Decades of dealing with her husband, Petya, and her son, Misha, have left her with a short fuse. They're a lazy pair, often drunk, squabbling with their friends and looking for a bottle. Slobs, she calls them, almost daily, with a snort and a roll of her eyes. And they nod, and smile apologetically, knowing she is the boss of this small, chaotic, hand-to-mouth household, tethered to a gentle hillside in a quiet, not-quite-forgotten corner of southern Ukraine.

But now these young Russian troops have arrived, on a drizzly afternoon in early March, roaring through the village, churning up her vegetable garden, and knocking down her favourite pear tree with their tanks.

'Motherfuckers . . .'

Svetlana is not usually given to swearing. But the word, and others like it, have followed the Russians like a cloud of summer midges as they've fanned out across Rakove village, hammering on steel gates with their rifle butts.

It is Wednesday 2nd March 2022, one week to the day since the Kremlin launched its invasion of Ukraine. And the nation's collective bloodstream is still pumped full of adrenalin, and outrage, and a cloying, nauseating sense of disbelief. It's like being woken from uneasy sleep, to find yourself in a deeper waking nightmare. Vast columns of Russian armour are advancing from Belarus in the north towards the capital, Kyiv, from the east into the Donbas region, and from the Crimean Peninsula across southern Ukraine, looking for a way to seize the entire Black Sea coastline.

Which is what has brought these Russian soldiers to Svetlana's cottage in Rakove, just outside the town of Voznesensk, with their guns and scowls and muddy boots, and this strange sense of entitlement. As if what they're doing here makes any sense at all.

An armoured personnel carrier has already crashed to a halt on top of the Martsynkovskyi's outside toilet, reducing it to rubble. Then a tank poked its barrel through the roof of one of three ramshackle barns. Finally, half a dozen soldiers came charging into the cluttered yard, threatening to shoot Zhulik, trampling mud onto the linoleum inside the cottage, and now threatening to shoot her.

'Why should I give you my phone?' Svetlana asks the Russian soldier. One hand holds her walking stick, the other rests defiantly on her hip. Her arthritic legs wobble slightly.

The soldier – a Chechen by the look of him – says they're collecting everyone's mobiles to stop them warning the Ukrainian military.

'Give me your phone. We're here to liberate you. To protect you.'

Svetlana won't let that go. She pulls her thick beige cardigan more tightly around her waist.

'From whom?'

'Fascists. Zelenskyy and his Nazis.'

She snorts in contempt.

'That's nonsense. You're just destroying everything,' she says, staring straight at him.

Which is what prompts the soldier to raise his AK-47, push it, almost politely, into Svetlana's stomach, and tell her he's going to count to three.

2.

One week earlier, at twenty-six minutes past five in the morning, the Mayor of Voznesensk rolled over in bed, grabbed his mobile phone and listened, in the dark, to the news that nobody – not a single person he knew in the entire town, not even the local defence forces, maybe nobody in the whole country – had believed possible.

'Understood,' said Yevhenii Velychko, already on his feet and looking for his clothes, trying not to let the pounding in his chest give way to a very natural instinct to panic.

Russian troops had just crossed the border. A horde of Russian missiles were already crashing into targets across the country, including the military airport some 15 kilometres south of Voznesensk. The Kremlin's invasion of Ukraine had begun.

Yevhenii was a slim, earnest, energetic 32-year-old; a former property developer with short fair hair and a quietly brisk manner of speaking, like pebbles clattering down a slope. He called his deputy, Andrii Zhukov, and they agreed to meet at the office as soon as possible. A few minutes later the mayor was in his car, driving through icy, empty streets as he drew up lists in his head.

Both men had spent the last weekend in the capital, Kyiv, attending a conference on the theme of 'Safe and Capable Communities of the Future'. It was the usual routine of local government, but the hall was filled with a new generation of young politicians and officials. Some were still wrestling with the corruption and cronyism of post-Soviet capitalism, but most seemed busier updating their social media pages and following in the nimble footsteps of Ukraine's unlikely new president, the former television star and comedian Volodymyr Zelenskyy.

At the conference there had been a session about security, and a stern talk about the need for local administrations to build up their volunteer home guards in the face of escalating threats from Russia – Putin's crazy rhetoric, all those troops massing on the border. But it felt abstract. Russia was obviously bluffing, whatever the Americans said. A speaker at the conference went out of his way to reassure everyone.

'There won't be a war. We're ready for anything, but don't worry. All will be well.'

★ ★ ★

Back home in Voznesensk, the mayor drove down October Revolution Street, then turned into the local council headquarters, a sturdy three-storey building, painted pale yellow. It was still pitch dark outside, and freezing. He was worrying about his wife, his 9-year-old son and 2-year-old daughter still at home. He'd need to get himself a gun.

Voznesensk – the word means 'ascension' – was a small farming town of well-tended single-storey cottages spread out around a neat central grid of Soviet-era administrative buildings and older, pre-revolutionary houses and churches. It seemed to have worked hard to preserve its architectural heritage – or maybe it was simply too much of a backwater to attract development. There was an old sports stadium, a lovingly curated museum, a busy market, several statue-clogged parks, and a railway station.

As Ukraine's economy limped away from the era of Soviet central planning, the town's leather factory closed down, along with the fruit cannery and a huge dairy cooperative. But in more recent years, the local grain industry thrived. Now, there were two sushi restaurants on the street in front of the mayor's office, as well as a small hotel, a well-stocked book shop, and a café selling beetroot soup and a dozen kinds of dumplings. It was an orderly, pretty town, distinguished by its position at the confluence of two rivers. At Voznesensk's edge, the big Southern Buh River – the country's second longest – is joined by a smaller tributary, the Mertvovid, meaning 'dead water'.

Yevhenii walked upstairs, past the fish tank in his outer office, and over to his desk. Minutes later, his deputy, Andrii, arrived, an IT expert with a pudding-bowl haircut and a background in medical systems programming. The two sat at the oval conference table on the first floor and began trying to contact their counterparts in towns closer to Russian-held territory, hoping to find out what on earth was going on. There was no point in trying to get hold of anyone useful in Kyiv, let alone in the military. It was hard to believe they had gathered here only the day before for a local council meeting about social grants.

Within an hour, almost a dozen senior local officials had arrived. The town's police chief, the hospital director, the head of the local defence forces. Mostly young, and an almost equal mix of men and women. A sign of the times. Everyone wore the same, wide-eyed, 'can-this-really-be-happening' expression.

Andrii called his wife. They were going through a divorce and she and their 3-year-old son were staying in a different town, much closer to the approaching Russian forces. He wanted them to come to Voznesensk, but she was scared, and insisted on staying put. As the room filled up, Andrii muttered what most people were thinking.

'I have no idea what to do now.'

3.

At about seven that same morning, a battered green Renault pulled into the car park outside the mayor's office. In the footwell, behind the driver's seat, lay an AK-47 rifle carefully painted in camouflage colours, a rolled-up foil blanket, a set of body armour and a backpack. The usual kit. Full combat mode.

The driver, a neat, stocky man with closely cropped fair hair, got out and greeted the others. There were a dozen of them. All armed and dressed in similar camouflage uniforms, like members of a local gun club. They were experienced volunteer soldiers, some active, others on leave or otherwise off duty. They arranged themselves into a circle around him.

'Everyone here?' he asked.

The man's name was Vadym, but he was known to everyone as 'Ghost.' He'd earned the call sign over the course of the past eight years, fighting the Russians in the Donbas, mostly around the town of Bakhmut – a place that would soon become famous for withstanding more than half a year of ferocious Russian assaults. Before the Russians invaded Crimea in

2014, Ghost used to dabble in farming. Later, he got involved in business, and football, and won a seat on the town council. But after he volunteered to fight, he found his calling as a kind of spy. Before long he was commanding a group of reconnaissance troops. He was good at second-guessing the enemy and crawling through fields to spot their positions.

'I guess it's in my nature,' he would tell people.

For a while it had seemed as if Ghost's life was settling down, with a new girlfriend at the beauty parlour in town and a teenage daughter studying in Poland. Like most of the men around him, he tended to adopt an attitude of weary, all-knowing cynicism about Russia, and he was ready for another fight. But even he hadn't foreseen a full-scale invasion.

The group set up a security cordon around the town hall. Within a few hours there were sandbags and rotas and patrols. But first, Ghost went to go and see Yevhenii, to warn him of what was to come.

★ ★ ★

Alarmingly, the Russians were already on the outskirts of Kherson, just 140 kilometres away as the crow flies. They'd crossed the giant Dnipro River. The next big city, Mykolaiv, was just a short distance to the west, along the coast.

Ghost leant over the mayor's conference table, jabbing his finger at a large map of southern Ukraine, talking through the risks, as he saw them.

Mykolaiv would put up a fight – Ghost was sure of it. At the very least, the Ukrainians would have time, over the next few days, to rig explosives on Mykolaiv's huge Varvarivskyi Bridge, across the Southern Buh. The bridge was 750 metres long, with a section in the middle that could be swung 90 degrees to allow boats to pass. If the Ukrainians blocked that crossing point, then the Russians' path to the Kremlin's key target – the great port city of Odesa and the headquarters of the Ukrainian navy – would be thwarted. At least for a while.

But then what? The Russians would need to find another way to cross the river.

The Southern Buh River snakes extravagantly as it makes its way north from the Black Sea, past Mykolaiv's old ship-building yards, its giant new grain silos, and through the elegant city itself. Beyond Mykolaiv, the river straightens out and slowly narrows, meandering through the placid countryside until it reaches Voznesensk. And it is only here, some 80 kilometres upstream, beside a new pier where grain barges dock, that there is another bridge across the Southern Buh.

The main road from Mykolaiv to Voznesensk – the P06, under repair in some places – runs along the eastern bank of the river. But anyone wanting to cross the Southern Buh itself first needs to cross Dead Water River.

'Here,' said Ghost, as he pointed to the map.

It was obvious. If the Russians planned to push further west to Odesa and beyond, they would have to come up the P06, take the bridge over Dead Water River in Voznesensk, and then turn left, crossing another bridge over the Southern Buh on the southern outskirts of town. If they did so quickly, and kept the momentum going, they would cut off the main road between the capital, Kyiv, and Odesa. In all likelihood, the Russians were heading straight towards Voznesensk at that moment.

And there was another reason why the Russians were, surely, focusing on this small, seemingly innocuous town. Thirty kilometres north of Voznesensk, the Southern Buh provides water for a hydroelectric power plant, and for the second-largest nuclear power station in Ukraine. If they seized the plant, with its three pressurised water reactors, they would have the country's entire energy system in their grip.

Yevhenii, Andrii and Ghost looked at each other. There was so much to organise, and no real sense of how much time they had. A few days. A week, if they were lucky.

They needed sandbags, and concrete barriers, and volunteers, and rotas, and bunkers, and secure communications, and food for the soldiers and volunteers, and an early warning system – a network of spies in the surrounding villages – and Molotov cocktails, and more guns, and a lot more ammunition. They needed to work out the most likely lines of attack. They needed to know if they would get any military reinforcements from a national army already grappling with a thousand different priorities. Above all, they needed to come up with their own plan – a plan which might enable a group of mostly amateur volunteers to defend their town against a full-scale Russian offensive.

Lurking behind it all was the knowledge of what they were up against. Plenty of Ukrainians were old enough to remember how the Russian army had destroyed its own city,

Grozny, not once but twice when fighting Chechen separatists in the 1990s. For the past eight years, they'd watched Russia's proxies fight in the Donbas. And they'd seen the news from Syria, where Russian artillery had methodically destroyed entire cities. The fate of civilians didn't matter to the Kremlin. The Russians would either sweep unopposed through the town or they would seek to level it.

Yet, at no point that morning did anybody raise the possibility of simply locking their doors and letting the Russian army pass through Voznesensk. If anyone had been considering it, they kept quiet. Instead, more lists were drawn up, priorities established, and any lingering sense of shock about the invasion was quickly buried beneath the many tasks at hand.

Ghost left the mayor's office, got into his Renault, and headed across Dead Water Bridge towards Rakove. It was time to start work.

4.

They're not much to look at – and they know it. A shabby parade of pot bellies, grey beards, baseball caps, trainers and tracksuits. The youngest of them is 18, the oldest are pensioners. Most of them have never held a gun before.

But here they are, on Wednesday morning, seven frantic days later, standing in a makeshift trench on the south-eastern outskirts of town, peering into the mist, taking turns with the binoculars, cadging cigarettes.

These thirty home guard volunteers represent Voznesensk's first line of defence, and the odds are not in their favour. As the hours slouch past, and the cigarettes run out, you can almost hear doubts rising, like nervous thought bubbles, from the trench. How much fucking longer? Is this just a futile gesture? Should we have got in the car and driven west, fast, like our neighbours did last weekend?

Valentyn, a 38-year-old lawyer, joined the home guard the day the invasion began. He's a cheerful, lean, unmarried man who has lived all his life in Voznesensk, close to his family and school friends. He recently adopted a pregnant stray cat and practises Brazilian jiu jitsu at least three times a week. But he's no soldier; he's used to dealing with legal disputes rather than warfare. To him, signing up had immediately felt like the right thing to do, but most of the others around him now only joined yesterday, when any last doubts about an imminent Russian attack vanished. Already, several of them have deserted, including one officer and someone on the town council. Some vanished from their positions here, in the cold, beside a derelict Soviet-era water pumping station. A few more slipped away this morning, after they received confirmation of the approaching Russian column, and the first dull explosions sounded behind them in town.

Valentyn can't wait any more. He pulls himself out of the trench – not really a trench, just a deep hole left by unfinished building work years ago – and goes to relieve himself against a nearby bush.

He doesn't know the names of most of the men in the platoon. A few are wearing camouflage gear. They were given AK-47s and a box of twenty grenades yesterday. Now they're supposed to stop an armoured column, or maybe several columns, from entering the city.

They chose this spot, a square of derelict industrial buildings with cracked concrete walls and broken windows, because of its view. From it you can see past grey, stubbled fields towards Rakove and the main road from Mykolaiv.

Everyone assumed the enemy would advance along the Mykolaiv road. But this morning there's confusion about which way the Russians will be coming. One of Valentyn's own relatives phoned him earlier to say he'd seen a huge column of Russian armour passing their cottage to the east of Voznesensk, near a town called Yelanets. They were on an entirely different road.

5.

Further up the same hill, where the ravine disappears into the fields like a ship running aground, three civilians stand in a huddle, lighting their first cigarettes of the day. Perhaps, they mutter, it wasn't such a good idea to come to work this morning. Maybe there's another bottle of vodka lurking nearby. They've already had a few shots.

Misha, Roma and Slavik all work, in one form or another, at Voznesensk's municipal dump. Most days, Roma and Slavik sift through rubbish in search of scrap metal they can sell to a recycling business in town. Misha has recently been given a job guarding the place. They've been friends from school days, inseparable except for those times when alcohol twists them the wrong way – twists Slavik in particular.

'I've got a screw loose,' he sometimes says, with an apologetic smile.

Since the first Russian invasion in 2014, it doesn't take much, just a drink or two, for Slavik to start talking about traitors in their midst, and to point a finger at his friends. They've fallen out too many times to remember, sometimes under Svet-lana's sceptical eye, while they're sitting in her courtyard.

Misha is Svetlana's son, and his parents' cottage is on the same hillside as the dump. He goes by the nickname 'Katsap'. The nearest English equivalent is probably something like 'Goat'. It's a disparaging Ukrainian word for a Russian man. But Misha has been called Katsap since he first moved to Rakove at the age of 9 and, since then, life has beaten him down enough to accept the name, almost proudly. He's 42 now, with a daughter living somewhere in a nearby village. She was taken away from him after his partner died and he started drinking more heavily. Now he spends most of the week up here, patrolling the dump's smouldering fields.

They hear the first explosions around 11 o'clock, muffled slightly by the low clouds. The man in charge at the dump has already warned them that a Russian column may be heading their way. Or maybe several columns. Misha and Roma take turns standing on an upturned barrel, looking to the north and east.

There is a casual, glorious, almost clumsy grandeur to the landscape of southern Ukraine – something about the scale of its features. Endless wheat fields stretch towards every horizon, wrapping vast, exaggerated contours. Sizeable towns, power stations, bridges, all look like miniatures, dwarfed by giant rolling hills, expansive rivers and deceptively deep ravines that unspool southwards towards the Black Sea coast.

'Tanks,' says Misha, pointing.

There must be thirty vehicles, at least. Maybe a lot more. Armoured personnel carriers, fuel trucks, rockets, lorries. Heading towards Voznesensk from the direction of Yelanets. The convoy stops on the brow of the hill, about a kilometre away from them.

Misha calls his mother. She starts to tell him she's planning to warm up some cabbage rolls for his dinner. He interrupts her, saying that the battle has started.

Suddenly, Roma is shouting.

'Down! Run!'

Bullets are zinging overhead. Roma and Slavik crawl through the dump, looking for a hiding place. They're both on their phones, calling anyone they can reach in Voznesensk to tell them the Russians are here.

But Misha is already moving south on foot, heading across the ravine's narrowing prow, and on towards Rakove, to his parents' place, earnestly wishing he hadn't drunk anything that morning.

6.

It's an arrow-straight 40-kilometre drive, due west, across dark, snow-speckled fields, from Yelanets to Voznesensk. On the outskirts of town, near the dump, the route passes a new solar plant with acres of glinting panels and the red-and-white steel girders of a television tower.

Earlier this morning, an eight-man squad from Voznesensk's small, permanent, defence unit drove up to an old warehouse just behind the solar panels, hid their cars, and set out on foot, looking for a good spot for an ambush. They are all professional soldiers, not like the volunteers at the water plant down the hill; and no doubt because of that, they've quietly managed to source a handful of NLAWs: next-generation light anti-tank weapons.

The British-made NLAWS are shoulder-launched rocket systems – incredibly lightweight, disposable, and almost childishly easy to aim and fire. The manufacturers claim the weapon 'can be deployed in around five seconds by a single soldier, day or night.' In the first week of the war they've emerged as the essential weapon for Ukrainian infantry trying to block Russia's advance.

At around noon, a 30-year-old officer – a Voznesensk local more used to setting up the occasional roadblock – steps out from the trees on the southern side of the road. Like the others in his unit, he's carrying two NLAWs.

He places one on the hard ground beside him and raises the other to his shoulder, squinting at the approaching Russian convoy. He pulls the trigger and is rocked back on his heels as the rocket blasts forwards. It roars along the road and hits a Russian truck loaded with perhaps thirty infantrymen.

The vehicle erupts in a flash of white-orange light, becoming a mushrooming inferno.

'Bullseye.' There's a murmur of approval. And no indication that anyone onboard the truck has managed to escape. The soldier does not stop to consider that. This is war. He drops the launcher and bends down to pick up his second NLAW.

7.

Like most of the officers in Russia's 126th Coastal Defence Brigade, 48-year-old Igor Rudenko had had an inkling that something big was being planned; something involving Ukraine. The lower ranks were being kept in the dark, and the official explanation for everyone was always 'exercises'. Nothing more. But by January 2022, the chatter in the crowded officer's mess had grown louder and more specific.

Tall, lean, straight backed and with hollow cheeks emphasising his Slavic bone structure, Igor looked like a model Russian soldier. But he had more reason than most of his colleagues to feel apprehensive about what was coming.

The 126th Brigade was based in Russian-occupied Crimea – the huge, diamond-shaped peninsula that bulges out into the Black Sea, about five hours drive to the south-east of Voznesensk. Its headquarters were on the edge of a town called Perevalny, set back from the resort towns and beaches, up in the hills close to the battle fields of the nineteenth-century Crimean War with famous names like Balaklava and Sevastopol.

In the previous weeks, an increasingly intense regime of inspections and exercises had taken place. The troops all heard the Kremlin's angry rhetoric about Ukraine on the evening news. But there had been no official update. Then, in late January, Igor's battalion, along with tanks, armoured personnel carriers (APCs), artillery, rocket systems – the works – was sent to eastern Crimea, close to the 'miracle' bridge to mainland Russia, which President Putin had opened back in 2018.

Now there were live fire exercises on cold, snow-dusted plains. Mortars, AK-47s, heavy machine guns. And then, on the 20th February, the battalion was told to move again, to the far side of Crimea, closer to the narrow neck, just 5 kilometres wide, between the peninsula and the mainland. And it was here, in a village called Slavnaya, that Igor and his fellow officers were shown the official order, from Putin himself, explaining that this was no exercise.

Immediately, the mood changed. The artillery battalion's ranks were beefed up by new arrivals, young conscripts, who'd been drafted in but told to pretend they were professional soldiers. Conscripts weren't supposed to fight outside Russian territory unless war had been declared, and this was going to be Putin's 'special military operation', not a war. Then extra kit was handed out. More ammunition, medical kits, tourniquets and a Soviet-era opioid drug, Promedol, which was used for the treatment of pain, along with morphine injections.

When Igor asked the division commander about their plans, he'd replied, 'If they're handing out the Promedol, we're off to war.'

On the 23rd February, Igor and his colleagues went into the nearest town to buy white paint. They'd been told to paint the letter 'Z' on their vehicles so that Russian aircraft could tell friend from foe. A few hours later, the convoy set off in the dark, heading north out of Crimea. Their orders were to advance about 80 kilometres to the huge Dnipro River that slices Ukraine in two. There was a key bridge at a place called Nova Kakhovka, about 80 kilometres east of Kherson. Igor's battalion was to help seize the bridge so that more convoys could cross and head towards Kyiv and along the coast.

At some point after midnight, Igor saw a red glow spreading on the horizon. The Russian bombardment had begun. Soon after, the convoy drove through what had been a Ukrainian checkpoint and they saw the first dead soldiers. The bodies of three Ukrainian troops lay near some barbed wire by the side of the road. Russian tanks took up positions nearby. It seemed clear the Ukrainian defenders had been caught by surprise.

There were plenty of reasons for members of the 126th Brigade to feel uncomfortable at that moment. For years they'd been told they were a purely defensive force, entrusted with protecting Crimea. Putin himself had said as much. They had no real sense of the scale of their operation, and no indication of its ultimate purpose. But for Igor, something far more personal troubled him, something that cut to the heart of this conflict.

Igor was Ukrainian. So were quite a few others in the 126th.

Igor had been born in a village on the Dnipro River, just upstream from the bridge he was now going to attack. He was a

Ukrainian man, with a Ukrainian wife and daughter. He'd once taken an oath to protect the Ukrainian state. Now here he was, part of a foreign army invading his own country.

How had it come to this?

* * *

Igor Rudenko spent most of his childhood on the Crimean Peninsula, home to the giant Soviet Black Sea Fleet. But by the time he turned 19 and decided to embark on a career in the military, the Soviet Union had collapsed and the Crimea had become part of independent Ukraine, so Igor began his military training at a Ukrainian academy. To some extent, the labels seemed trivial. Ukrainian, Russian, Soviet – what mattered was having a decent career. Meanwhile the military system was still going through the slow, often painful process of working out which bits of kit – which battleships, which bases, which guns – belonged to which newly independent nation.

Brinkmanship was applied. Deals were eventually signed, and Russia finally ended up with the bulk of the Black Sea Fleet, along with an agreement that the Russian military could continue to hold on to its ports and bases in Crimea until at least the middle of this century.

By 2014, Igor was married, with a 3-year-old daughter and a promising career in the 126th Brigade, in command of field communications for a company. But Ukrainian politics were changing fast. A young generation was itching to escape Russia's sphere of influence, to break free of an authoritarian Kremlin's clumsy embrace and join the European Union.

Moscow's increasingly heavy-handed attempts to prevent that had built to a climax. In the space of a few, extraordinary weeks, Ukraine's pro-Russian President was forced from power by a popular uprising, and Russian troops seized the Crimean Peninsula.

At that point, Igor made what he would come to think of as 'a huge mistake'. Rather than abandoning his brigade, and his career in the Crimea, he simply swapped sides, pledging a new oath of allegiance to Russia. Several thousand Ukrainian soldiers did the same. For the most part, there was no great ideological debate about it. People had families and homes on the peninsula. A shared Soviet history. It was easier just to stay put.

Igor later claimed they'd been 'zombified' – won over by years of Kremlin propaganda that promised them better pay, better kit, better accommodation and a standard of living two or three times higher than in Ukraine. And it all seemed plausible. Ukraine was in political chaos, governed by corrupt oligarchs, and wrestling with its place in the former Soviet empire. Why not switch to a resurgent Russia?

It took a few years for the truth to sink in. Igor was promoted, and Russia did invest heavily in the Crimea, which became a showcase for Russian military might. But the promise of better accommodation never materialised. Then Ukraine cut off a key canal which provided water to the peninsula. There was rationing. Prices shot up. And those Ukrainians who'd stayed behind soon suspected that their Russian colleagues despised them as much as their former colleagues back in

Ukraine. They were trapped. Igor saw the situation for what it was: a hoax, and a farce.

But still, others had remained optimistic. The brigade's commander was also Ukrainian, but he despised the pro-Western politics in Kyiv, the nationalism, the sheer speed of change there, and the sense that the military was being asked to betray its glorious Soviet roots. After all, the 126th Brigade had fought in the Battle of Stalingrad. It had helped drive the Nazis out of Crimea. And now, under a Russian banner, it was becoming a proper fighting force again.

★ ★ ★

Four days after Russia's invasion began, Igor's convoy had crossed the Dnipro River and was preparing to swing west towards Kherson. Other units from the 126th were also converging on Kherson from the south. Ukrainian troops, still reeling from the shock offensive, had begun pulling back towards Mykolaiv. Within hours, Kherson – once a huge economic hub, a ship-building port left struggling since the 2014 invasion – would fall to the Russians.

But it was not easy going. Ukrainian drones and mortars targeted Igor's unit. They'd lost several APCs. And then, on the night of 28th February, outside a small village on the vast plain north-east of Kherson, the column was surrounded, and pounded for hours, with great accuracy, by Ukrainian artillery.

Early the next morning, Igor and the ten other surviving soldiers crawled out of a nearby forest. Some were injured.

Filthy, lost and surprised to be alive, they were met by a group of Ukrainian farmers with shotguns.

'Don't shoot us, lads. Don't shoot your own people,' Igor said, knowing how strange, how absurd, how offensive, the words must sound.

One of his own soldiers, exhausted and on edge, fired a short burst from his machine gun, but it missed the approaching Ukrainians.

'Don't shoot,' Igor was now shouting. There was a pause.

'Who is the commanding officer? Let him come forward,' one of the farmers shouted back.

Wearing a heavy green camouflage jacket with the Russian flag prominent on its left arm, Igor raised his hands and walked onto the road. Within a few minutes it was over. He and the other soldiers quietly surrendered their weapons and were taken prisoner. Their convoy had been wiped out and dozens of soldiers killed or wounded.

Within days, Igor would be sitting behind a long table in a conference room in Kyiv, a prisoner of war, still in his bulky uniform, a sheen of sweat on his forehead, sighing deeply as he addressed a crowd of journalists and camera lenses, and looking like a man desperate to drag a weight off his chest.

'I'm a citizen of Ukraine,' he began. 'My soul hurts. I beg your forgiveness.'

8 .

'Mum. Give him the phone. Don't be stupid.'

Misha has run from the town dump to the edge of Rakove, all the way to his mother Svetlana's cottage. On the way, he noticed more Russian armour on the main road by the river's edge. Gunfire rang out from near the water plant. And he saw that Russian vehicles had started moving north through the village itself.

Misha quickly made up his mind to surrender. He walked across the open fields behind his parents' house, and on spotting the first group of Russian soldiers he raised his hands above his head. At gunpoint, they pushed him towards Svetlana and his father, Petya, already standing together beneath the bare vines that shade the courtyard in the summer. Svetlana is arguing with one of the soldiers, refusing to give her phone up.

'I will not ask again. Give me your phone and lie down on the floor. We are here to protect you,' says the soldier.

'Mum!' Misha shouts at her. Her shoulders slump.

Now it's Misha's turn to hand over his own mobile phone. He realises, too late, that he has not deleted his call history.

'02,' says the soldier, peering at the screen. 'Police.'

'Oh God, my son. Please don't kill us,' says Svetlana, weeping, one hand on the red shawl tied around her head. From his distant look and the clumsy way he moves his weight, she can tell Misha has been drinking. And now they're going to shoot him. It's like a scene from one of those war movies.

But the soldier sees it too – the drunkenness. He can tell that Misha is no threat.

'Do you want me to shoot him?' the soldier asks Svetlana, his voice thick with sarcasm.

'Oh, Misha,' Svetlana shakes her head. They're sitting on the ground now. Another soldier takes the phones – they already have bags full of them – carries them round the corner and throws them onto the mud in front of a tank, which edges forwards, noisily, to crush them into the ground.

'We're not barbarians. You'll be all right if you do as you're told,' says the soldier guarding them.

Some of the Russians are filling sandbags with mud. Someone else has set fire to bundles of straw to provide cover for the snipers' positions on the cottage roofs. A helicopter flies low overhead.

'One of ours,' says a taller soldier, presumably in charge. He's busy with a radio.

'Are you staying here then?' Svetlana asks.

'We'll leave in the morning,' he replies.

'Please don't bomb our house,' says Svetlana.

Another Chechen soldier pushes past, lugging a wooden ammunition box into the yard.

'If your guys hadn't attacked us on the main road we wouldn't have had to come through here. And now we've got casualties. Do you have bandages? Syringes? Antibiotics?' he asks.

'Nothing. Just my blood pressure tablets. This is a small village. The doctor only comes once a week,' Svetlana replies, forcing herself to be polite.

And now the soldier gestures towards the gate, ordering the three of them, Svetlana, Petya and Misha, to leave. Now.

'Find a basement. The battle is about to begin.'

As the three of them head down the hill, they hear the thud and clack of helicopter blades. Ahead of them, past Rakove, beyond a couple of empty fields and a row of spindly trees, the Southern Buh River takes a slow, casual turn. On the far side, there's a large pale meadow, more than a kilometre wide. Behind it, the land rises sharply into woods. Beyond that lies a small Ukrainian air force base – Martynivske – which was hit again by Russian missiles early this morning.

As the Russian column comes under fire to the north, a fleet of military transport helicopters begins dropping off Russian paratroopers. Over the course of the next few hours, about two hundred soldiers will land here – a chilling sight for Voznesensk's defenders.

Ghost soon gets a phone call alerting him to their arrival. Someone from a nearby hamlet is already spreading the word, and, with it, a host of new questions. What are the Russians planning? Is this a single event, or will more paratroopers soon be delivered to other fields around the town? There are checkpoints on all the main roads into Voznesensk, but what if the Russians are planning a much bigger assault? If they're surrounded, there's no way the town's defenders can fight on all sides.

Behind all these questions is an even bigger sense of uncertainty. The war is only a week old. It's still too early to know exactly what the Kremlin is planning to do, how far it will go. At this stage, the flawed assumptions, the arrogance, ignorance and clumsy organisation that underpin Putin's Ukrainian plans have not yet become clear.

The arrival of paratroopers on the outskirts of Voznesensk has simply reinforced what Ghost and others have been saying all week. That this little town and its rusty bridge over Dead Water River are key targets for Russia – important enough to put together a big and apparently well-coordinated operation. The Kremlin is clearly determined to push along the southern coast of Ukraine, at all costs.

9.

The last time the mayor posted on his official Facebook page, he gave his followers a rather dull account of the conference he and Andrii had attended in Kyiv. Photos showed the two of them wearing lanyards and posing stiffly alongside other delegates, with a brief note about 'the implementation . . . of the decentralisation of power'. Ghost had responded, leaving a comment on the site, asking what real steps would be taken for the urgent business of civil defence, and the mayor replied that training would be organised, garnering one 'like'.

The next time the mayor updated his page was in the hours after Russia's invasion began. Yevhenii posted a short video message showing himself flanked by Andrii and Spartak, the head of the regional council. The three stern young men were seeking to project calm to the people of Voznesensk, but you could see in the tension in their shoulders, the effort required to hide their shock.

Kyiv had already been bombed, and so had Kharkhiv and Mykolaiv. Russian troops were streaming across Ukraine's poorly defended borders. So much for Putin's bluff.

Yevhenii was soon strapping himself inside some black, lightweight body armour, worn over a green fleece. He was given a pistol and a holster, and the blue armband, which all the town's defenders would soon put on. But should the three of them – the town's political leadership – stay together, or separate in case one of them was killed? Was it safe to use mobile phones? Should they stay here, in the administration building? And where should they sleep?

They quickly agreed to move their headquarters somewhere safer – there was a cellar two blocks away that had been renovated. Next, they would need to close the town's schools, and start organising trains to evacuate the many families who were in a hurry to head west, away from the advancing Russians. The town's population was thirty-five thousand, and there were about a hundred and eighty-five thousand more in the surrounding countryside. Andrii was put in charge of coordinating a plan for anyone wanting to leave town by train.

And yes, there were 'some people' who really should have stuck around. Businessmen, local officials, even friends, who quietly packed their bags and left Voznesensk in its hour of need. That would be on their consciences, and doubtless there would be a reckoning at some time in the future, when all this was over. Nothing dramatic, perhaps, but people would remember who did what. Still, it was astonishing to see how quickly everyone else quietly pulled together. In their new cellar headquarters, the administration had been overwhelmed with offers of help.

The civil defence unit organised a rota to man check-points around town, particularly on the main road south-east towards the big city of Mykolaiv. More than a hundred local men volunteered for duty. During the first Russian invasion in 2014, concrete blocks had been put out to slow down the traffic. Now more were added, and bunkers built on the roadsides. Companies hauled sand and gravel into town from the local quarries to block roads and make sandbags. Dozens of local children, freed from school, joined the production lines, filling bags and helping the adults to fortify key buildings. The town's restaurants and kitchens churned out thousands of meals and delivered them to checkpoints and to the yards where welders were turning out dozens of crude steel tank traps. Other civil-ians were filling glass bottles with petrol, then plugging them with cloth to make Molotov cocktails.

You wouldn't call it fun. But few could deny an over-whelming sense of purpose, the thrill of a community suddenly bonding, intensely, over a shared cause.

Yevhenii, Andrii and Spartak became inseparable. Like one organism, one person, was how Andrii thought of it. They came up with their own code names: Yevhenii's father had once served in the army and had been known as 'Mongol', so the mayor now borrowed the nickname.

On that first night Yevhenii and Andrii slept – for no more than a couple of hours – at a canning factory near the town centre. They changed locations every night. In the end, the three of them, including Spartak, decided it was best to stick together round the clock. Far easier than having to update each other by phone every few minutes.

One morning, after a night at a leather factory on the western outskirts of town, they stopped their car near the main road. By now they had a permanent bodyguard with them, codenamed 'Wolf'. On the far side of the road, they watched a man get out of his car and hurl something into the undergrowth, then drive off fast.

'That doesn't look right,' said Andrii.

The four of them combed through the grass and quickly found a small, electronic device. They couldn't tell what it was; maybe some kind of tracking device, a way to steer Russian missiles towards particular targets. Andrii got on his smart phone to check Google maps and saw someone had planted a virtual flag at the same spot and left a comment – 'Great place to relax. Unrivalled mud baths.'

There was no way to be sure without expert help, but 'mud' sounded like some kind of code word. Maybe a place for an occupying army to position weaponry. At first, they couldn't decide what to do with the device. Put it back or destroy it. In the end they smashed it with a rock, then hid it where they'd found it, covered with earth.

'Let's get out of here,' Andrii told the others.

★ ★ ★

For most of the first week after the Russian invasion began, the mayor and his team assumed the worst and prepared accordingly. In the general, nationwide chaos it was still impossible to reach anyone who mattered in the military. Ukraine's army, caught off-guard, was struggling to stop the Russians advancing on so many fast-moving fronts that it seemed certain they would not have the resources to assist one small provincial town. It appeared increasingly likely that the local leadership would have to defend Voznesensk alone, with just a handful of local soldiers and whatever volunteers they had scraped together.

There were a lot of holes in their defences, but Yevhenii was particularly worried about Dead Water River. The natural barrier that seemed to protect the town was in fact permeable. Upstream from the bridge, there were shallow areas where the invaders could cross with their tanks. The Russians didn't know about these yet, but all it would take for that to change was one local sympathiser deciding to tell them.

There was no way to make the river deeper. But perhaps they could make the banks higher? And so the town's leadership came up with a new plan: they would build ramparts. A couple of local farmers brought in dozens of truckloads of earth, then a bulldozer began piling it along both riverbanks and shaping it. The resulting muddy brown fortifications looked almost like an ancient Roman fort. No one was entirely sure if it would work. But it felt good to be doing something practical.

Then suddenly, a little after lunchtime on the Monday, less than two days before Russia's 126th Brigade would reach the outskirts of Voznesensk, the mayor had received a brief phone call to inform him that the Ukrainian army, specifically the 2nd Battalion of the 80th Airborne Assault Brigade, was on its way.

Military support was coming. Just ten minutes later, a convoy of Ukrainian army trucks crossed the main bridge over the Southern Buh River and drove into town, shuddering to a halt on the roadside near the administration building.

Feeling a huge weight had just been taken off his shoulders, Yevhenii jumped into his car to go and meet them. A short, sturdy-looking soldier with narrow eyes and a close-cropped beard walked over to the mayor and they shook hands warmly. The battalion commander was polite, but to the point.

'If you want this town to survive, then listen to me,' he said, in a soft, solemn voice. Yevhenii nodded vigorously.

The commander's name was Oleg Apostol, and with him were some three hundred professional soldiers, who'd been fighting the Russian invaders for the past week and had only just escaped from behind enemy lines near Kherson.

Oleg's code name was 'Formosa'. The 80th Brigade had been fighting Russia since 2014. A quietly popular soldier, with a reputation for listening to advice, Formosa had risen fast through the ranks to head a whole battalion in 2018.

He had picked his call sign years ago, when he was still a keen young cadet in Lviv, dreaming of a career in the special forces. He had taken it from the name of an island – he couldn't remember whether it was off the coast of Japan or China, but he liked the sound of it.

On 24th February 2022, Formosa and his forces had been at a training camp close to Mykolaiv. But with no imminent invasion expected by the Ukrainian government, they weren't in the right place to defend the country from attack. They'd immediately been ordered to advance towards the Russians in the fields between Crimea and Kherson. If they'd been a day or so quicker, they might have clashed with Igor's column from the 126th Brigade as it pushed north from the peninsula. Instead, Formosa was ordered to bring his forces close to the Antonivskyi Bridge, just upstream from Kherson.

The Ukrainians were determined to hold the bridge. But the invading army had tanks, powerful armoured vehicles full of infantry and air support. It was an impossible task. Within hours, the 80th, along with many other units, were forced to retreat, pulling back into Kherson as Russian forces swept across the Antonivskyi Bridge and began to encircle the whole city. The Ukrainian military commander quickly decided there was no choice but to order a withdrawal from Kherson. Later, there would be angry questions about why the city was abandoned so quickly, and even allegations of treason. But at the time it seemed clear that to avoid a complete rout the soldiers needed to slip through enemy lines at night, falling back to new defensive positions around Mykolaiv.

And now, a few days later, the 80th were beside another bridge, this time in Voznesensk, and charged with defending it against the same invading force that had just brushed the Ukrainian army aside around Kherson. The outlook was not good; despite the early setbacks that had seen Igor Rudenko captured, and his unit crushed, the remainder of Russia's 126th Brigade was already advancing from the direction of Mykolaiv in three columns.

'We have no tanks, and not enough NLAWS or Javelins to destroy all their armour,' said Formosa to Yevhenii. But he did have dozens of artillery pieces – sturdy, Soviet-era howitzers with a range of up to 20 kilometres, including a handful that were self-propelled, with tracks like a tank. The mayor, grinning broadly, did not even try to hide his relief.

'What do you need from us?' he asked.

'We need beds, food and some equipment – car batteries, diesel,' Formosa replied.

Andrii started making calls. Ten soldiers could stay in his empty flat, for starters. Soon he found seven other places, including the basement of the old House of Culture, beside the mayor's office. Beds and meals were organised. For his head-quarters Formosa chose another basement, just across Council Street and below a rather elegant old bookshop. It was close to the mayor's temporary new subterranean office.

Quietly, pensively, Formosa began to sketch out the beginnings of his plan.

First of all, they needed to slow down the approaching Russian columns, and even destroy them, if they could. Ghost and the local home guard had already set up roadblocks on the two likely approaches into Voznesensk, but Formosa now ordered his men to lay mines on the roads, 10 to 15 kilometres out of town.

Secondly, they would have to fight the Russians inside town. There was no other option. Outside Voznesensk, the countryside was mostly open, the roads straight, with few options for ambushes. The Ukrainians might manage to destroy a few Russian tanks, but they had no armour of their own. It would be a massacre.

'We will have to lure them into Voznesensk,' Formosa said. The mayor raised a hand.

'What about civilians here? What about the buildings?' He could picture the town being reduced to rubble.

But Formosa was adamant. He left the cellar and walked through town, towards Dead Water River and its sturdy old bridge. This was the place. This was where they could set the trap for Russia's tanks, funnelling them down the hill from Rakove village, across the river, then cutting them off by destroying Dead Water Bridge. After that, his men and their rocket launchers would do the rest.

There were risks involved. But Formosa could see no other option.

* * *

A loud, ecstatic roar sailed from the cellar doorway and out onto the quiet street. It was Tuesday afternoon and inside the mayor's bustling new offices the staff had already rigged up connections to a dozen or so pre-existing security cameras around town. They didn't begin to cover the whole of Voznesensk, but the images, visible on a monitor in the office, gave them a decent sense of what was going on. They even had one up by the solar farm, with a clear view of the main road east. And the calls and texts kept coming in from villages closer to Mykolaiv.

'I'm in Nova Odesa. We just saw a Russian convoy heading your way.'

The mayor's team had eyes everywhere, civilians feeding back information about the progress of Russia's 126th Brigade. Part of the convoy had already split off, moving further north and seizing another town called Enerhodar, along with its nuclear power plant. But the bulk of the Russian force, perhaps six hundred soldiers, was still heading towards Voznesensk. Formosa's three hundred Ukrainian troops would be outnumbered at least two to one.

The news that triggered roars of excitement in the mayor's office was that Formosa's artillery had just destroyed one entire Russian column. Maybe a dozen tanks and other vehicles were now out of action.

Andrii was hugging people around him and punching the air with his hand. A keen football fan, for a moment he felt the kind of delirium associated with winning the World Cup – giddy, ecstatic. But then Formosa, on the other end of the phone, reminded them there were still at least four hundred experienced and heavily armed soldiers heading their way.

10.

It's already past noon on Wednesday, but there's no way of knowing that from the leaden sky over Voznesensk. Smoke is still billowing from the remains of at least two Russian vehicles, hit by the local soldiers' NLAWs.

As they slip away on foot towards town, the Ukrainians can't quite believe how easy it has been to catch the invaders by surprise. It's as if they just expected to charge straight through Voznesensk without a hitch. They hadn't even bothered to send their infantry to patrol the side streets on the outskirts of town.

But the Russians are regrouping, moving off the Yelanets road and heading south instead, past the solar farm, and down towards the other main road into Voznesensk, near Rakove and the water pumping station, where thirty home guards including Valentyn, the local lawyer-turned-volunteer, are still waiting in their trench.

A few minutes later, Valentyn finally spots the Russian convoy. He's heard the explosions and realised the Russians have followed a different road and come under Ukrainian artillery fire. Now the convoy is passing within 400 metres of him. His heart thumps in his chest. And then, for a moment, his mind wanders. He thinks what this week might have been like without the war; what he would be doing right now. Fishing, perhaps. A couple of months ago, he narrowly failed one of the new tests the government introduced as part of its shake-up of the criminal justice system and quit his job in the local prosecutor's office soon afterwards. It had been a lot of work, much of it tedious, for the equivalent of a hundred pounds sterling a week. He was considering a new career when the invasion began. This was not what he'd had in mind.

Valentyn's commander, a 29-year-old computer programmer named Zhenia with a year's military experience as a former conscript, picks up his radio and calls in the Russians' position as accurately as he can. No one is sure how much good that will do, and whether the Ukrainians have sourced enough artillery shells to do any real damage. The home guardsmen still assume they'll be cannon fodder, brushed aside by the might of the enemy's professional soldiers.

Just below them, they can see the back of a Shell petrol station, then a lorry depot, and behind it, further down the hillside, the slate-grey swirl of the Southern Buh River. The pumping station itself is spread out over a big area, with two-storey buildings, a water tower and a clear line of sight across the surrounding countryside – still frost-hardened and wintry.

For a while, the Russians pause on the road by Rakove. There are tanks, armoured personnel carriers, artillery, Grad rocket launchers, trucks; an intimidating display of military hardware.

Valentyn hears a sharp, grinding roar, and then the column begins advancing towards town. He's only just slipped back into his trench after another pee. He can see hand-painted Zs on the Russian vehicles. And almost immediately, the convoy is on the road below them, a hundred metres away.

Suddenly, there's a huge explosion, and the front tanks burst into flames. Then another screeches to a stop. Within seconds, the rest of the column is already beside the Shell garage and desperately trying to disperse. The Ukrainian 80th Brigade's howitzers, positioned about 3 kilometres away, have found their target, pounding the area around the garage.

In the chaotic aftermath, two Russian tanks and two armoured personnel carriers swerve up the hill towards the pumping station, and as they turn left, some of the home guardsmen open fire.

'Stop that!' Zhenia, the platoon commander, knows there's no point firing bullets at an armoured vehicle, but the firing continues, in long, wasteful bursts. Then someone throws a grenade. Then another.

The tanks brush aside the flimsy gate and enter the station grounds. Within seconds, Russian soldiers are clambering out of the APCs and moving fast on foot, surrounding the buildings to cut off any chance of a retreat.

Valentyn and Zhenia both have four magazines for their rifles, each with thirty bullets. Firing on automatic, each magazine will last just 3 seconds.

Beside Valentyn, an older man whispers that he can't see properly. He clambers further out of the deep trench, ignoring Valentyn's urgent warning, and almost immediately takes a bullet to the chest. Blood gushes out, soaking his casual clothes. Valentyn tries to stem the flow, but he has to keep fighting too. His body is awash with adrenalin, but, rather than fear, he now feels an odd sense of calm and purpose.

Another man slumps back into the trench with a bullet through his collar bone. Then a third home guard is hit, fatally, in the head. Zhenia is busy applying a tourniquet to someone else, swearing under his breath as the injured man cries out in agony. The situation is clearly hopeless. What were they thinking? Amateurs, pensioners, kids, playing at warfare.

'Guys, we're with you.'

A Russian voice suddenly hurls the strange words across no-man's land. The tone is earnest, almost indignant.

'We're with you.'

It's a call of comradeship. The enemy is trying to negotiate, to explain to the Ukrainians that they're brothers, fellow Slavs; that, in truth, they're on the same side, that they've come to liberate them from fascism.

Valentyn feels like laughing – these guys really believe the nonsense they've been fed. All the lies, the propaganda about Nazis. He can see the Russians in their uniforms now with white armbands. They look like elite troops – maybe paratroopers – tall, well trained, well armed. Valentyn pushes his last magazine of bullets into place, takes aim, and fires another burst.

Earlier, Zhenia, the platoon commander, positioned a handful of guards inside one of the pumping station buildings to give them a different line of fire. But they've already run out of ammunition. Now he calls out to Valentyn, asking him to get on the walkie-talkie and explain their situation to their headquarters in Voznesensk.

'Three dead, two wounded,' Valentyn reports in.

'How long can you hold on there?'

'Perhaps five minutes,' Valentyn replies. He knows it's probably even less than that. There's a pause, then the message comes back – they can surrender, but they should consider what they've already heard from the frontlines around Kyiv, from places like Bucha, where surrendering troops have reportedly been executed en masse.

'So be aware, they may just shoot you anyway.'

By now, the gunfire around the pumping station has almost stopped. The Ukrainians have all run out of ammunition and grenades. Valentyn smashes his walkie-talkie against his gun to destroy it. An older volunteer comes over to explain that he can't surrender – he's spent time fighting the Russians in the Donbas and they'll see as much from his documents. He'll be shot, for sure. He shakes Valentyn by the hand and makes a run for it, straight down the hill, towards the petrol station. There's an almost comic moment as a tank lurches towards him, as if to catch him, and then he's across the road, and out of sight. He's made it.

The rest of the group are already starting to surrender, emerging from the trenches without their weapons, holding their hands above their heads and walking slowly, towards the enemy. Valentyn is overcome by a sense of deep longing – for his family, for his life. He's sure he will either be shot or sent to prison in Russia. Then he joins his comrades.

The next few minutes are a kind of savage chaos.

'Fucking lie down!'

'Fucking dogs.'

The Russians are screaming at them. Some have knives out, threatening to slit their throats. Others are pointing pistols.

'Why did you fight?'

The soldiers are not just angry but outraged – shocked that anyone would dare to confront them. Even now, after a week of fighting, the Russians are still waiting to reach the real Ukrainians – the ones who need liberating, the ones who will be grateful, who will throw roses in front of their tanks.

'In here. All of you. Now.'

The Russians push everyone inside one of the buildings, then strip the men of their jackets, phones and any other equipment.

'Not you two. You're coming with us.'

Zhenia and Valentyn are led away from the others and taken to a separate room.

'Where are the rest of your forces?'

The interrogation begins with a few slaps. A punch. But the two men know very little about the army's plans for Voznesensk, about where the 80th Brigade's artillery are positioned, what tactics they have for blocking the bridge, Formosa's whole strategy.

Valentyn starts talking, slowly, politely, trying to show the Russians that he's eager to cooperate, but that he doesn't have the information they want. His lawyer's training is kicking in.

'You must understand, we're just volunteers. We were told to hold our positions here, that's all.'

He speaks in fluent Russian, using his best text-book accent, and he can see that the Russians are losing interest. They're distracted, anxious, still surprised by the resistance they've encountered on the outskirts of Voznesensk. And, it seems, increasingly uneasy about what lies ahead of them.

1 1 .

The plan was to meet at seven that morning, one street back
from Dead Water River, before the battle started. But Serhii
has overslept, and by the time he is up and dressed it is nearly
11 o'clock on Wednesday morning and his friends have already
gathered in the centre of Voznesensk.

It will be Serhii's 22nd birthday tomorrow. Half a dozen of
his former school friends are waiting for him, all in their late
teens and early twenties now, and entirely unprepared for what
is about to happen. They've spent the last few days in a kind
of giddy frenzy, slapping each other's backs, swearing to do
whatever it takes, and assembling Molotov cocktails in the yard
outside Serhii's mother's home, a couple of blocks behind the
mayor's office.

An air raid siren starts up again; plaintive and chilling; a
slow howl of dread drifting across the town. They've already
heard explosions from the airbase, a long way to the south.
But soon the first Russian shells are hitting Voznesensk itself,
crashing into an apartment block and tearing holes in the walls

of the handsome municipal swimming pool. Russian tanks are firing, seemingly indiscriminately, from out towards Rakove.

Serhii and his friends gather outside the rusty green gates of number 53 Tamaschyshyna Street, which runs along the south-eastern edge of central Voznesensk. There are office buildings on one side and two dozen cottages on the other, backing onto the meadows and reeds along Dead Water River.

'Fuck!' Serhii and his friends drop down behind a low wall as a tank round crashes into the top floor of an apartment building further downstream. The boom seems to circle around them. This is suddenly getting real.

Three Ukrainian soldiers, members of the 80th Brigade, stop briefly, taking shelter behind a brick wall, then continue to walk further up the road. The Ukrainians have placed one of five sniper teams, each composed of a shooter and a spotter who can also direct mortar and artillery fire, on top of a three-storey building at the end of Tamaschyshyna Street. From the roof, the two soldiers can see straight across the bridge, to where four Russian tanks have just come into view, perhaps four hundred metres away, advancing down a gently sloping road towards the river.

The tanks are part of the same giant convoy that was hit by NLAWs on the outskirts of town, then came under fire again near the Shell station. While some sections of the convoy have pulled back into Rakove in disarray, another squad of vehicles has pushed ahead, straight down the main road into Voznesensk.

Serhii and his friends know nothing about the sniper team on the nearby roof. But they can hear the rumble of armour and can tell the tank fire is getting closer. Adrenalin races through them. They grin, wildly, at each other as they scramble through the gates of number 53, hoping they can find somewhere in the back yard which might offer a view across the meadow and the river towards the Russians.

It is now twenty to two in the afternoon. The owner of the cottage, a retired fireman, escorts his wife and disabled son down into their small cellar. Then he comes back out and briefly stands beside Serhii, intending to go inside and get a blanket and pillow for his wife. A small dark cat, hesitant at first, races past the front gate.

Serhii is still working out what to do with his life. He recently graduated from university in economics, but since then he's been doing odd jobs – building work, car repairs and the like. In his spare time, he's a keen boxer and keeps pigeons. He's a tall, popular guy with a strong chin, even features and thick eyebrows. He's the youngest son of Anna, who still dotes on him to an embarrassing degree.

Half an hour earlier, Serhii and his friends met the mayor near the bridge, where various volunteers were handing out Molotov cocktails and grenades. There was a bit of a scramble. They each managed to grab a grenade, silently picturing the moment they would hurl it at a passing tank.

The shell that kills Serhii is travelling at nearly four times the speed of sound, which means it takes about a third of a second to cross Dead Water River, smash through a thin garden wall, and splinter against the grey concrete side of number 53.

There's a deafening blast, and a cloud of white smoke punches its way across the road.

Perhaps the soldier inside the T-72 tank meant to aim a fraction to the left, and up, at the sniper. Maybe he panics, as the Ukrainians defending the bridge open fire with all manner of weapons. Or maybe he isn't aiming at anywhere in particular.

The explosion is captured, at 1:43pm, on the black-and-white video of the security camera attached to the side of the tall building opposite. The shell hits the owner of the house first, taking his head clean off. Despite days of searching, it will never be found. Immediately behind him, Serhii is torn apart.

12.

It is a strange name for a river – Dead Water.

By the time it reaches Voznesensk, easing down the eastern edge of town between the neat administrative centre and the hillside cottages of Bolgarka village, it is 50 metres wide. But there's not much of a current, and large patches of the river are clogged with reeds and coated with a sheen of algae. It's tempting to imagine its name refers to a stagnant, brackish stretch of water, a feeble tributary of the mighty Southern Buh.

In fact, Dead Water is, for most of its length, a rather lively stream, twisting and leaping through steep canyons on its way south. And it has at least two rival origin stories and possibly many more.

Around three hundred years ago, Cossack horsemen established a winter camp on the banks of Dead Water. The Cossacks were becoming a formidable political and military force, challenging the Ottoman Empire's hold on the fertile plains north of the Black Sea, and this area, close to a ford further upstream, held significant strategic value. According to one theory, there was some sort of clash between the Cossacks and the Ottomans near Dead Water. The Cossacks slaughtered their enemy and threw their bodies into the stream, clogging the waters with the dead, and earning the river its unusual name.

Another, earlier version, tells a slightly different story with a similar conclusion. A local community living near the river wanted to take revenge on a group of invading Tartar forces from the Crimean Peninsula. Using herbs or berries, they made a poison and poured it into the river upstream from a Tartar encampment.

If you go back a good few centuries, there are other theories – of dead Scythian rulers being pushed, in boats, into the river for their funerals; and of the ancient Greek historian, Herodotus, mentioning a river in the area with an old Iranian name, which directly translates to 'dead water'.

Voznesensk took longer to earn its name. It was only in 1795 that Catherine the Great issued a decree turning a small settlement into a town, as the Russian Empire muscled its way towards the coast. Old etchings show smartly dressed Russian cavalry in precise formations, conducting exercises outside Voznesensk in 1837. A century later, after changing hands repeatedly during Russia's civil war, local farms submitted to Soviet collectivisation and the famines that accompanied it.

In 1941, the Nazis occupied Voznesensk but not – according to some versions – before the Soviet defenders had blown up Dead Water Bridge. The Nazis then rebuilt it, reportedly using Jewish gravestones from the local cemetery to construct the new foundations. In 1943, the Gestapo executed more than sixty partisans behind the walls of the local dairy factory.

Today, the same bridge is still in use, eight decades after it was reconstructed and then abandoned by the retreating Nazis.

13.

Two blocks from the bridge, on the wide, tree-lined corner of Kirov and October Revolution streets, bullets are fizzing overhead, smacking into walls and shattering the front of a small supermarket. Shards of blue-tinted glass slip and crash to the pavement and clouds of dust drift across the intersection, towards a group of soldiers crouching behind the walls of an old Tzarist-era cottage. A car alarm is bleating, non-stop, somewhere to the left.

'Sniper!'

Ahead, up in Bolgarka village, two or three Russian snipers are making it hard for the Ukrainian forces to move around. Why can't someone take them out? It feels like it's been hours.

'Stand closer to the wall.'

'But I've got to see what's fucking happening.'

The words are shouted out, above the crackle and boom of the fighting, but the tone is calm. Profane, but calm; soldiers' chatter.

'Fuck it, I want to piss. I know it's a war, but I still need to piss.'

The Ukrainians here are a mixed bunch. There are professionals from the 80th Brigade, some local police and territorial defence forces, and a handful of volunteers like Alexander Moskaliuk, a stout, lively man who owns a nearby shop. He's brought his rifle along, but he is busy filming his reactions to the fighting around him on his mobile phone.

'I can throw a Molotov cocktail.'

'A cocktail will do fuck all,' someone mutters.

A block away, to the east, October Revolution Street begins to rise, gently, as it prepares to cross Dead Water Bridge. The bridge is an old, steel truss design, with a plain tarmac road over the top, grey metal fences on the edges, and a crowded lattice of rust-coloured beams underneath. It's a sturdy, unremarkable bridge, the sort of thing you might drive across without noticing you were suspended, until you caught a flash of reflected sky, a bright shimmer of water amid the meadows and reeds on each bank.

On the far side of the bridge, three Russian tanks and an armoured personnel carrier are just coming into view, having made their way down from Rakove village. The tanks are sleek, bristling, alien creatures, covered in a sort of explosive hide made of a mosaic of green boxes that can each blast outwards to destroy an incoming projectile on impact. Their tracks dig into the tarmac and their long barrels swivel menacingly from side to side. Amid them, the APC looks worn and shabby, covered in filthy-looking sandbags placed by the crew as an extra layer of protection. But the APCs and tanks are all formidable war machines, refurbished with the latest equipment, including thermal imaging systems.

'Why did they fuck off like that? Where the fuck did they go?' One of the Ukrainian soldiers shouts across the road to a colleague, sheltering behind the wall of a computer shop. He's talking about the town's police, who've suddenly moved away without telling the others.

'Fuck. There were plenty of them. Maybe they've been ordered to approach from the side? I guess we'll know when we hear shooting.'

'We need a machine gunner over here. Get across to this side of the road,' says another voice.

There's a deep explosion, as a tank round slams into a building somewhere close but out of sight. No one even flinches. What they've just heard is the sound of a shell hitting the wall of 53 Tamaschyshyna Street, killing two men – a retired fireman and 21-year-old Serhii Ahapytov.

★ ★ ★

'Ready for action. Wait for the command.'

'Nobody's going anywhere.'

A Ukrainian soldier from the 80th Brigade, squatting with his back against the wall, suddenly stands up and glides out, with balletic grace, onto the broad pavement along October Revolution Street. In one fluid movement, he hauls the metre-long tube of a rocket-propelled grenade launcher to his shoulder and leans forward, almost imperceptibly, like a seaman bracing for an oncoming wave.

'Firing!'

The soldier shouts, pulls the trigger, and before the rocket has exploded, he's already moving back towards the shelter of the nearby wall, eyes still fixed on his target across the bridge.

'Yeah! You little beauties!'

Alexander Moskaliuk is watching from behind the farmers' store, a wide grin spreading across his face as he stands up, peers a little way around the corner, and screams out from beneath his black hoodie like a football fan watching the winning goal.

'Yes! You hit it!'

Another incoming tank round explodes, much closer than the last one. Later, they'll learn that it killed a local volunteer, a junior officer. Ghost and his reconnaissance team were standing next to him on a corner, closer to the bridge, but moved away about a minute before the shell landed.

'That was a tank, firing at us. No big deal,' says Alexander, crouching again, his grin almost as wide, talking into his phone camera.

'We're alive! Look over there! We're alive!'

It is now, as the Russian tanks start moving closer to the bridge, that a cloud of uncertainty begins to swirl around the Ukrainian defenders. They have a plan – Formosa's plan. But it's all happened so quickly, with the 80th Brigade arriving on Monday, all these different armed groups taking part, and so many messages shuttling between them all – on walkie-talkies, on WhatsApp, Viber, Signal. And now a fundamental tactical disagreement has come to the fore. When should they blow up Dead Water Bridge?

★ ★ ★

The 80th Brigade's intention was to draw the Russians into Voznesensk. The deeper the better. An ambush of sorts, disguised as a retreat. Once ten or more Russian tanks have crossed the bridge into the town centre, the defenders will be able to pick them off, one by one, working on foot, hiding in backstreets, firing their shoulder-launched rockets from apartment windows and cellar doors.

A Ukrainian army engineering platoon arrived here on Monday from Kyiv, consulted briefly with Formosa and the mayor, and then quietly set about rigging the bridges with explosives. And not just Dead Water Bridge. They also wired the railway bridge that crosses high over the Southern Buh near Rahove, another section where the railway line crosses a main road in the centre of town, and also the road bridge south across the Southern Buh.

Yesterday, the defenders decided to blow up both sections of the railway line, there and then. No sense in waiting. But there's still a lingering disagreement about Dead Water Bridge. The mayor and his team have been involved, from the start, in the military plans for defending Voznesensk, but now the 80th Brigade is very much in charge. Yevhenii has continued to argue against bringing the fight into town, concerned that too many civilians are still here and that too many apartment blocks are occupied and could make tempting targets for Russian tanks.

It's not as if anyone wants the fighting to take place on the far side of the river, in Bolgarka, either. There are also plenty of civilians there. But it's better, the mayor insists, to blow up Dead Water Bridge well before the Russians have a chance to cross it.

Formosa and the 80th are adamant. At least the front half of the first Russian column should be allowed across, then it can be trapped and surrounded and destroyed entirely, rather than risk letting all that armour retreat to find another way across.

But what if something goes wrong with the explosives? What if they leave it too late and the Russians manage to secure both the bridge and the town? Last week, in the initial scramble near Kherson, a young Ukrainian soldier blew himself up with the aim of destroying another bridge seconds before the Russians swept across it. They won't leave it that late this time.

A huge explosion thunders around the town – far deeper and longer than the blast of a tank or artillery shell. It's the sort of blast you feel in your rib cage, your eyes, your skull.

'Christ. Was that our aviation?' One of the Ukrainian soldiers a block from the bridge looks up, wondering if a fighter jet has dropped a bomb on the advancing Russian column.

But it's Alexander Moskaliuk, the shopkeeper, who guesses right.

'They're blowing up the bridge! Beautiful! That's it. They've blown it up!'

A huge column of grey-white smoke rises high over Voznesensk, is picked up by a slow breeze and guided gently towards the Southern Buh. When the clouds clear, the impact is immediately visible. The entire central section of the bridge juts downwards like a giant grey tongue. There are deep cracks in the creased tarmac where it now hangs vertically down. One big chunk of steel latticework has been thrown sideways into the river, while another smaller section at the nearer end of the bridge remains precariously in place. The explosion has done its work.

'Fuck,' says one of the 80th Brigade soldiers.

'Is the bridge completely destroyed?' a local defence force soldier asks.

'I don't know. It was your guys who blew it up.'

'They blew the bridge up too soon. Shit. The Russians were supposed to enter the city.'

There's a pause. No gunfire for a minute or so, as everyone seems to adjust to what's just happened. Then a call comes through, and the soldiers from the 80th Brigade spread the news.

'The boss is very angry. Very fucking angry.'

There are shrugs and smiles, and crude comments about Vaseline and rape, and the sort of punishment they, or someone, can expect when this is all over. But the deed is done. Dead Water Bridge has fallen – too soon, in the eyes of some. Russia's convoy has been blocked, but it has also avoided a potential trap.

★ ★ ★

This is what happened.

When the Russian column first approached the bridge, some of the town's defenders were too quick to open fire, effectively springing the ambush too soon. The Russians fired back, killing one of Formosa's soldiers on the fifth floor of a nearby building. And somehow, amid the subsequent explosions, the mortar, artillery and tank fire, a long, thick wire cable was disconnected. The cable coiled down the edge of the road, into the grass verge, and on towards a detonator that was then attached by more wire to some 200 kilograms of explosive TNT, carefully packed around the girders in the centre of the bridge.

The demolition squad, hiding in a nearby building at the other end of the wire cable, called in to Formosa.

'There won't be an explosion,' said an officer, explaining the problem.

At which point, a member of the local defence force stepped in, unannounced, and on his own initiative. He crawled over to the broken wires, reconnected them and, out of fear that it was their only chance, he manually triggered the explosives himself. The strength of the blast and its accompanying shockwaves could have killed him – maybe should have killed him. But, somehow, he staggered away, heavily concussed.

And now the bridge is down.

'They can't come through here anymore,' says one of the 80th.

'So, what the fuck are we standing here for then?'

'Okay, let's move on. We need to outflank them. Let's head that way.'

There's still a Russian sniper or two up on the ridge in Bolgarka, behind the broken bridge, and there is still a larger battle to be won. The bridge is broken, but if the Russians realise how shallow it is further upstream, they could clear a path through the mayor's improvised earth ramparts to ford it in a tank. If they seize the town, they could put in a new pontoon bridge. But Formosa has already prepared for that, dispatching some of his men to the meadows along the riverbank.

The soldiers peer round a corner, then sprint fast across October Revolution Street.

14.

'Don't shoot!'

The words come out in a squeal of panic, shouted across a street in Bolgarka district, at around 4 o'clock that same afternoon. A few dozen metres away, taking shelter behind a wall, the Ukrainian soldiers are not quite sure what to make of it. Are the Russian soldiers surrendering, or are they just confused?

'Don't shoot!' The words are shouted again.

Seconds earlier, another Russian armoured car was hit by a rocket. Three soldiers jumped out of the vehicle but came under immediate fire from the Ukrainians. It was the same team of eight men who attacked the Russian convoy with NLAWs near the television tower earlier in the day.

Now, one of the Russians is badly injured and another soldier – presumably a young, frightened conscript – is begging the Ukrainians to stop so he can drag him to safety. But a third Russian has just opened fire.

So, the Ukrainians fire back, reluctant to treat this like some kind of gentlemanly game. Fuck that.

It's been a strange few hours in Bolgarka. Now that the bridge is down, it has become the focus of the battle. Russian forces are hoping to secure the place in order to regroup and launch another push towards the town centre. Some of the Russian soldiers clearly know how to fight well – they've already established sniper positions high up in a local church. But others have no clue, and no wish to be here. And then there are those who seem more interested in looting local houses; raiding fridges, grabbing whatever they can find.

Ghost's original plan, backed by Formosa, was to block some roads with concrete and rubble in order to funnel the Russians down towards Dead Water Bridge. It seemed to work early on, but now Russian tanks are simply crashing through walls and finding ways around the obstacles.

Bolgarka is an old neighbourhood of single-storey cottages with small orchards, high walls and wood stoves. It has barely changed in a century. And while some residents have already abandoned their homes, those who've stayed behind – many of them elderly – seem to be gripped by a mood of profound stubbornness.

'Put your fucking hands in the air!' a Russian soldier shouts.

He and two others, heavily armed and wearing green combat helmets, have just broken their way through the gates of a cottage, to be confronted by a defiant couple in matching blue sweaters. The pair – man and wife – are advancing towards the soldiers across the forecourt. Neither of them have any intention of raising their hands.

'Why should I? This is my house,' says the man, gruffly.

One Russian soldier fires a short burst of automatic gunfire in the air. The family dog has already sniffed the mood and trotted away to safety, but the couple stand their ground, arms by their sides, and even edge towards the soldiers as they continue to shout. It's a strange sight. The Russians begin wrestling with their consciences and with their actions here, in a country they've been assured would welcome them as liberators. The last week of fighting has made them aware of some of the flaws in that theory. They seem to be struggling to accept their true role as invaders, with all the contempt and thuggishness that the word implies.

'Fuck off. Go to hell,' the woman shouts. Slowly, as if pretending that this is what they intended from the start, the soldiers start to back out. In under a minute, they've exited the gate and are walking down the muddy street outside.

15.

Back on the hillside of Rakove, the Russians have just let Svetlana, Petya and Misha go. They shuffle out of their gate, past the soldiers, and past the now-silent dog Zhulik, still chained in the corner. Their neighbour's gate has come off its hinges, kicked in by Russian troops. They turn left and walk together through a landscape of muted greys and the palest yellows, along the rough path that leads past the cemetery and down the hill.

Somewhere nearby, a multiple rocket launcher, a Grad, is firing towards town. There's a rhythmic woosh as each missile passes overhead. Svetlana's legs are aching. Her back too. Petya walks slowly behind her, scratching his stubbled face. An armoured car roars past.

Svetlana is thinking about money. What will happen if their cottage is destroyed? The previous, ancient owners lived there since before the Great Patriotic war. They once told her, just before moving out, how the Nazis had chosen Rakove as a base, setting up their headquarters in a nearby house close to the ravine and using their own cottage cellar to store ammunition. It feels as though history was repeating itself.

Petya still hasn't got his pension. And Svetlana has given up hoping that she'll ever sort out the bureaucracy needed to get hers. They had sold one of their last cows a year back, just to pay some fine to some official at a rabbit warren of an office in Odesa.

They turn right just beyond the walls of a solid, square, almost windowless cottage. The Zegurovs' home. On hot summer afternoons, their neighbour Mikhail Zegurov can be seen, bare chested and darkly tanned, his tangled grey hair down to his shoulders, with all his weight on his one good leg, wielding a scythe in the field below like some mad ballet dancer. But for the most part, the couple have become invisible. His wife never comes outside anymore, even to take milk to sell in town. She's a drunk, people in the village whisper. Her man was once in the army, he fought in Afghanistan. Over the years the crude fence around their home and garden has been shored up by plastic buckets, a wooden pallet, scraps of metal and lumps of stone. It's hard to see how anyone can get in or out anymore.

Here we are, thinks Svetlana. Old and poor and forgotten. An archipelago of stranded, pensionless pensioners. And now this.

The crack of a sniper's bullet echoes off the cottage walls. Is it one of ours or theirs? In the distance, from far across the broad partially frozen Southern Buh River, they can hear the buzz of helicopters getting steadily louder. And closer, near the main road, a bright orange flicker by the petrol station tells them that something is on fire.

Svetlana and her two men hurry down the hill to join two other families who have taken shelter in a deep cellar not far from the post office. A Russian shell has crashed through the roof of the village clinic. In the hurry and madness of it all, no one has brought any food or water. Now there are perhaps twelve of them, squatting on boxes or on the dirt floor in the fast-approaching dark, cold and barely talking, waiting to see what daylight will bring.

16.

Soon it is night. The home guards at the water pumping station are all POWs now, sitting huddled in one room, sharing a few blankets, saying little as the hours pass. There's fighting underway just over the hill towards town, in Bolgarka. The Russians are in control of large parts of the neighbourhood, but they're pinned down, scared to fire their own weapons in the dark in case they're targeted by Formosa's increasingly accurate mortar and howitzer teams. And now they need fuel. A Russian officer comes in to make the strangest announcement.

'We need a hundred litres of diesel. So, we need two volunteers. Two of you,' says the officer.

The deal, if one can call it that, goes like this. If any two of the prisoners are prepared to drive one of the Russian trucks, find some diesel, and bring it back to the pumping station, the whole platoon will be released. But if those two prisoners fail to return, the rest of the men in the platoon will be shot in the yard outside. There's no negotiation involved. In the dark room, after a long pause, two hands go up. Valentyn, the lawyer-turned-volunteer, doesn't know their names, but he knows there's a good chance they'll be killed by their own side if they venture into Bolgarka.

The two men are taken outside.

An hour and a half later, there's a sound of grinding gears outside as a truck drives back through the broken gates. There's no time for the volunteers to explain where they've found diesel. Maybe they syphoned it from a garage, or took it from friends, or stole it from somewhere else. But the Russians stick to their deal. The prisoners are told to stand up and are escorted out of the building. They're free to leave and immediately sprint away, into the dark.

All except two men. Zhenia, the platoon commander, and Valentyn, who the Russians believe to be his deputy.

17.

In the dark of an unfamiliar cellar, Svetlana's thumb brushes the callouses on her hand. She can feel the knife, feel the steady downward force required, feel her toes cramped inside those rubber boots. It's like turning the page of a photograph album.

She was almost sixteen when she started work at the meat processing factory on a vast Soviet state farm. Her family had moved there a year earlier. This was back in 1976. Svetlana finished her vocational training at the factory school and went straight to work. Her mother had a job in the milking plant and her father drove a tractor. She was the oldest of six children – the other five still went to school.

Svetlana's title was 'butcher, de-boner, 4th category'. Each day she sliced her way through two tons of meat. Heads, jaws, pork backs, ribs, shoulders of beef. The firm downward tug of metal carving through flesh. A row of young girls wearing chainmail under their white aprons and endlessly sharpening their knives. All those cuts and callouses. Their hands became tougher than leather. Standing in a cold, damp room for eight hours a day. No wonder her legs ache now. But she enjoyed the work, the companionship, and the certainty of a life mapped out. A Soviet life. No chance of unemployment, no need to try harder than the girls on either side of you in the factory. Not much food in the shops. A quiet cynicism about the whole grand system, with its rituals and heroes and sullen discipline. They had one proper holiday a year, spent tinning and pickling vegetables from the family's small garden. Tomatoes, cucumbers, strawberries. She worked at the factory for fifteen years and might easily have carried on for fifteen more.

Back home, under her bed, Svetlana has a plastic bag full of old albums. There's one favourite photo, taken in the dazzling snow outside the factory. She and three friends, squinting and smiling. Thin woollen coats with sheepskin cuffs covering their overalls. It was the 8th March – International Women's Day. They had a mug of vodka each, topped up with lemonade.

Beside her now, in the gloom, her son is fast asleep. Misha. Always some new disaster. Yesterday, amid the drama of an imminent Russian attack, he went into Voznesensk to try to sign up to fight. He wasn't sure they'd accept him, almost 40 now, and with his criminal record. But the man told him, 'Why not – the home guard will still take you. They'll do the paperwork, and you can go to war.' A cause for celebration. Misha and his friends found another bottle, and so here he is, hung-over, unshaven, clothes filthy from the dump, and still not signed up.

18.

'Lights off! Turn the bloody lights off!'

It's now a little after 10 o'clock on Wednesday evening, and a solitary car is driving towards the centre of Voznesensk from the north-western outskirts. The mayor's deputy, Andrii, is at the wheel, and beside him, in the passenger seat, is a security guard. Yevhenii and Spartak, the local council leader, are in the back. They've kept to their rule of moving to a new location each night and have just spent the last few hours in a cramped guard's hut in the courtyard of a struggling pig farm, trying to keep warm beside a fire, taking turns to lie on a small mattress.

Over the past few days, Andrii has become a kind of one-man-shop for the military, sourcing spare parts from local businessmen and organising food supplies. He even found a boat – within 15 minutes – for some soldiers from the 80th who wanted to cross Dead Water River and attack several armoured personnel carriers in Bolgarka.

Now they're driving into town again to meet Formosa, to find out what else he might need from them, and where the battle is likely to move next.

They see the Russian helicopter before they hear it. It can't be more than a couple of hundred metres away, skimming over the treetops, then suddenly releasing a dazzling display of bright decoy flares designed to confuse heat-seeking rockets. It's a sleek attack helicopter, known as the 'Alligator', with two sets of giant blades, and a bristling display of guns and rockets beneath two stubby wings.

'Shit! Shit!' At the wheel of the car, Andrii has managed to turn the lights off, but he's panicking now, and ignoring the order to drive off the road and hide the car behind a nearby tree. Instead, he jams his foot on the break and simply stops in the middle of the street, beside a petrol station forecourt. And now they wait, hardly breathing, watching the helicopter, wondering if they might possibly have time to dive out of the car if they see a muzzle flash, and knowing the answer. The helicopter's powerful cannons can fire a hundred armour-piercing bullets every second. They could tear the car and its contents to shreds.

'Of course,' Spartak will recall later, 'we were all shitting ourselves. We're human. We're allowed to get scared.'

Maybe the pilot hasn't seen them. Maybe he's looking for more promising targets. But a few seconds later, the helicopter roars past them, overhead, then swings to the north and back across the dark silhouettes of Voznesensk.

19.

It's well past midnight now. Zhenia and Valentyn – the two remaining home guardsmen in captivity – are lying on their backs on top of a Russian armoured car, shivering, as they're driven through an icy mist and down the main road towards Rakove. Valentyn can't stop thinking, angrily, about the other men in their platoon. When they were released, they raced off without taking their three dead colleagues with them. Later, they'll explain that they thought the Russians might have laid explosives under them. But that seems unlikely to Valentyn. The others were just in too much of a hurry to get away.

The vehicle judders to a halt, then lurches across the road to help another armoured car out of a ditch. The two prisoners struggle to cling on. Their hands have been taped together in front of them. Then someone loads a dead Russian, in a black plastic body bag, beside them, and a wounded soldier clambers onboard too. Both APCs turn off the main road and up the track towards Rakove.

Valentyn can tell they've been brought to some kind of headquarters. There are several tanks, mortars and artillery pieces outside a cottage near the top of the hill. They've arrived at Svetlana's home. The two prisoners are dragged off the vehicle and someone ties their feet together with more tape. As they lie on a patch of mud and grass, one of the Russians bends down to whisper something in Valentyn's ear.

'I'm going to cut your balls off.'

They're hauled to their feet and dragged towards the wall of the cottage. A dog barks behind them.

'Get ready,' says a different Russian voice.

At that moment, in the murky predawn light, both men believe they're about to die. They are standing now, backs to the wall, with at least three soldiers pointing their guns at them. Valentyn thinks earnestly about his life in Voznesensk, recalls his mother, and then, in a fleeting moment of bitter regret, wishes that during the battle at the pumping station he'd killed more Russians.

'Stop.'

The Russian commander comes out of the courtyard. A lieutenant colonel. He stands in front of the two men and grabs Valentyn's chin.

'Look up. Look me in the eyes,' the colonel says.

Zhenia is shivering. It's impossible to tell where this is going. The colonel steps back and looks at their clothes – their jeans.

'These are not military. Not Ukrainian armed forces.' And then the colonel adds the same, quietly fervent phrase that the guards have heard so many times over the last few hours.

'We're all Slavs.'

And with that, the soldiers grab them and pull them through the gates. The courtyard is crowded with wounded soldiers, with more arriving all the time, and medics working out who to treat, in what order. They can still hear shelling in the distance, and it seems clear the battle isn't going well for the Russians. The prisoners try not to catch anyone's eye, but there are still insults thrown at them – 'Nazis', 'paedophiles'.

'If we stay here, we'll be torn apart. Better to sit in the barn,' Valentyn says to the commander, who nods.

As they're being taken across the yard to a shed behind the cottage, the two prisoners notice a civilian – an older local woman, in a beige cardigan. Valentyn briefly catches her eye. A major is now escorting them, and he seems less aggressive than most of the other soldiers, then he explains why. He's a Ukrainian too, from Poltava, serving in the Russian army. The three of them look at each other, and the major shrugs.

Then a wooden door is dragged open, and Zhenia and Valentyn are pushed inside.

★ ★ ★

It's dark inside the shed, but as Valentyn's eyes adjust, he can make out two pale faces amid piles of wood and farm implements near the back. There's a moment of silence, then a cautious 'hello', and soon the four of them are whispering to each other. The two seated men are Russian soldiers, members of the 126th Brigade. They're under arrest for disciplinary offenses and are being held here, in deep disgrace.

One of the Russians explains that he's a 19-year-old conscript from Rostov, just across the border.

'They told us we were going on exercises. Then they sent us to war instead,' he says, indignantly.

The commander of his platoon selected him to drive an armoured car into Voznesensk, right at the very front of the first Russian column.

'The first in the convoy always gets hit. The first vehicle and the last vehicle. Everyone knows that,' he says.

Which is why the conscript panicked. As the convoy was approaching the outskirts of Voznesensk, shortly before it came under fire, he deliberately swerved off the road and tried to crash. Then, as other vehicles started to overtake him, he continued attempting to sabotage his own APC by driving it into a ditch, then into the side of a house. Now he's being held here, braced for some sort of punishment.

A few minutes later, the shed door opens, and two more men are shoved in.

★ ★ ★

When Svetlana's son, Misha, decided to rush home from the municipal rubbish dump, his friends Slavik and Roma stayed put, first hiding in the small trailer that Roma sometimes uses to keep warm, and then – after two Russian APCs broke through the front gates of the dump – crawling across a field and settling into the undergrowth near a walnut plantation.

They stayed like that through Wednesday afternoon, listening to the explosions, wondering if Voznesensk had already been captured. Darkness fell, and then, around midnight, they decided to go in search of food.

'Hands up!' Roma and Slavik had barely walked for 30 seconds before gunfire erupted around them. They dropped to the ground and tried to crawl, bullets hitting the earth beside their heads. And now, two Russians were standing over them, prodding them with their rifle butts.

'We're nobody. We're homeless people, working on the landfill. We're thirsty,' Roma was babbling.

By torchlight, the soldiers stripped them almost bare, inspecting their shoulders, looking for bruises that would indicate they'd fired rifles – that they were soldiers. They told Roma to shut up, then they blindfolded the two men, marched them through the woods and bundled them roughly onto the back of an APC.

'Fuck. Shit,' Slavik hissed as the vehicle slipped and jolted over the rough ground. They were lying on top of each other, still blindfolded, with sharp metal edges digging into them.

After about 10 minutes, the vehicle stopped. Roma could feel the phone he'd hidden in his sock drop out as they clambered down from the APC.

'He's got a phone. It's broken,' said the soldier.

'Why did you break it?' asked another voice. Roma and Slavik were on their knees now, still blindfolded, and Roma could feel a knife at his neck.

'Your guys broke it, not me,' said Roma. He could smell the soldier behind him – stale sweat, diesel, cigarettes.

'You're fucking lying. Let's cut their heads off.'

'These guys are civilians. Let them live. Put them with the others.'

Then hands grabbed them by the arms, dragging them, one by one, across the mud, and throwing them into the increasingly crowded shed attached to Svetlana's cottage.

20.

Thursday morning arrives, grey and quiet at first. Svetlana's joints ache as she clambers up the step from the cellar.

'Oy,' she sighs.

She, Petya and Misha start to walk up the hill – a tarmacked road for the first few yards, then a dirt track for another kilometre or so – back to their house. It must be about seven in the morning, and they're all cold and hungry and are hoping they can find something to eat, and some warm clothes. It's worth the risk.

Mist hangs over the river behind them. The main road is full of Russian troops – a sniper has pulled bricks out of a wall and is poking his rifle through the hole. Some trees have also been cut down to give a clearer line of sight.

'I have a feeling they're going to kill us on this path today,' says Svetlana. But they keep walking – drawn, almost without thinking, back to their home, even though it means another encounter with the Russians.

As they pass below the cemetery, they see a big mortar, half a dozen armoured vehicles of various types, and a few shallow trenches in the field outside their cottage. They can hear the grumble of a generator inside.

Arriving at the cottage, Misha is abruptly grabbed by two soldiers.

'On your knees, bitch,' one shouts at him, a gun at his head.

'But you saw us yesterday. You checked us. Show him your documents,' Svetlana says. And almost as quickly as they pounced on Misha, the men shrug and walk away.

'My boys are hungry. Your fridge is empty,' says a Russian officer – a tall man with a potbelly and the code name 'Skull'.

Svetlana feels, once again, like she's walked back onto a film set. Filth is everywhere. Outside their front door, there's a man sitting in a chair, with most of his clothes cut from him, bandages on his feet and chest, and an intravenous drip suspended from a vine. Another soldier is slumped on a bucket by the well, and a third is moving around the courtyard on crutches. She has to supress the instinct to tidy up, to clear away the bandages, to mop the blood and mud from the front step.

Inside, there is blood everywhere. Thick and dark on the kitchen linoleum. Bloody boot prints through the whole house. And more Russian soldiers, lying everywhere. On the floors, on Svetlana's bed, in Misha's room. From the doorway she can see blood on a white pillow and a dark blue mattress. Another casualty lies on the sagging couch in the hall. But her collection of teddy bears still sits on a windowsill, waiting for her grandchildren to visit. Overnight their home has been turned into a field hospital. Medics are busy with some of the injured – mostly shrapnel injuries, by the look of the deep, jagged wounds. It's hard to find a space to step without treading on someone. The front door has been taken off its hinges and is now being used as a stretcher for a pale young soldier with a bandaged head.

The sniper shots they heard last night came from a water tower on the ridge to the north. Now Russian snipers are firing back from nearby. It's a straight line of sight across the ravine. On the walk up, Svetlana saw soldiers inside her reclusive neighbour Mikhail Zegurov's ramshackle compound and wondered if they'd been helping the enemy. Feeding them, perhaps. She wouldn't put it past those two.

Inside her own home, she manages to grab a coat and a couple of blankets. And now their cat, Sonya, comes strolling across towards her, weaving through the bandages and casualties. Svetlana picks her up and walks towards the garden, gesturing at the other two to follow her. Petya says nothing. He speaks less and less these days.

Then again, her husband was never much of a talker. Stubborn but quiet, he's three years older than her, born in north-west Ukraine. He came home from Soviet army service and spotted Svetlana one afternoon, playing volleyball with his sister, who worked at the meat plant's 'knitting' line, tying up sausages with string. Petya came over, bold as brass, and said, 'One day I'll marry your friend.' And then he stuck to it. He was handsome back then. Lean and fit, and patient, with a strong chin, and a strange surname – Martsynkovskyi. Some people said it was Polish, but he swore his ancestors were all Ukrainians.

They got married when Svetlana was 18. A simple ceremony at the local registry office was followed by a reception with sliced sausages, vodka and dancing. It was the tail end of the Brezhnev era, and life was fine. Slow, predictable and constrained. But fine. Their first child, Misha, was born seven months later and the family were soon given their own house near the factory. They raised pigs and chickens to supplement their income, and quietly pocketed meat from work. Everyone did the same in those days – the communist system was quietly devouring itself. When Brezhnev died, there was a whole week of national mourning. Svetlana had to cancel her birthday party at a local disco. She liked to dance.

'Old farts,' she called Brezhnev and the grey men who succeeded him. But at least things still worked, in a creaking sort of way.

Then came Gorbachev, in a hurry, shaking things up, even trying to ban alcohol. Petya's cousin was living near Chernobyl when the nuclear reactor exploded. She needed a bone marrow transplant but went to the doctor too late, and there was no donor to be found. By then, everything else was spinning out of control. In 1991 the 'old farts' staged a coup in Moscow. In its aftermath, Ukrainians voted overwhelmingly for independence. In Russia, Yeltsin took the same course. And within weeks, Gorbachev was out of power and the Soviet Union had collapsed.

By then, Petya had a job at a factory. The factory was privatised, and Petya used his voucher of shares to buy a car, then borrowed more money at a steep interest rate, got involved in a scam to sell meat in Moscow, was swindled out of everything, and then crashed the car.

'Mistook the accelerator for the break. Bloody idiot,' Svetlana never tires of reminding him, flicking her neck with a finger to indicate that he'd been drinking at the time.

Petya's passenger ended up halfway through the front windscreen and Petya crushed his ribs on the steering wheel. The car was a write-off. They were lucky to survive. Within a few dizzying months, the gangsterism of post-Soviet capitalism chewed them up, swallowed their savings, and spat them out on a hillside above Rakove, in a cheap cottage they spotted in a local newspaper.

Now, as the three of them set off back down the hill to the cellar, they see a soldier standing guard outside a brick shed at the back of the house, an old workshop.

'Prisoners?' Svetlana asks.

'A bunch of them,' replies the Russian.

'You bastards,' Svetlana mutters to herself.

21.

There are six of them in the shed now.

The soldier standing outside keeps opening the door, peering in, and striding over to kick Zhenia and Valentyn and wake them. At other times he shines his flashlight in their faces. It goes on for hours.

'Why are you giving them a hard time? Give us some water,' says Roma.

'Sit.'

'We are sitting.'

Another soldier comes in and begins looking at Roma's long socks. He's wearing two pairs.

'Those look good,' says the man. Judging by his Asiatic appearance, he's from eastern Siberia.

'Are you so poor you can't afford your own?'

'Something like that. I'll take the top pair,' the soldier replies, pulling them off Roma's feet.

Eventually the main guard seems to relax a bit. He speaks to Zhenia.

'We took Odesa without firing a shot. We're heading to Kyiv. How far away is it? Two hundred kilometres? Fifty?'

The prisoners quietly glance at each other and shake their heads in contempt. Most of these Russians don't have a clue what's going on, why they're here, or where here is.

'No,' Zhenia replies. 'You still have nine hundred kilometres to go.'

'Fuck. We've only just got here and we're already getting the shit kicked out of us. Fuck knows what's waiting for us in Kyiv. If we ever get there.'

22.

Lying in a ditch not far from the Shell petrol station, peering through his binoculars, Ghost can see and hear the 80th Brigade's artillery starting to work more methodically, targeting Russian positions around Rakove village and further south, in the wide meadow across the river. Russian paratroopers are now pinned down and making desperate calls back to base, asking for the helicopters to return and evacuate them. It seems the paratroopers were simply supposed to wait until the Crimean 126th Brigade had seized the town, and then they would help secure it. They've not moved since their arrival on the far side of the Southern Buh River, and no other paratroopers have been dropped anywhere else around Voznesensk.

Behind him and his reconnaissance team, Ghost can hear the occasional crack of a Ukrainian sniper's bullet passing overhead. He and his men take turns to nap, 20 minutes at a time, heads resting on the frosty ground. Each man slips into sleep almost instantaneously.

Surely, the Russians will bring in more reinforcements. That seems logical to Ghost, and to everyone else. But right now, as evening approaches on the second day, the Russians are clearly struggling. One column tried moving further north, to attack Voznesensk through another suburb, but Formosa's artillery quickly put a stop to that. Now the Russians have started to pull out of Bolgarka, and dozens of their abandoned armoured vehicles litter the main road, supplies spilling out of them like the guts of gored animals.

There is no whistle blown, no siren, no indisputable sign to indicate that the momentum is shifting. But late on Thursday afternoon, as another wave of light drizzle wafts across Voznesensk, a surge of confidence seems to infect the town's defenders. It's different to yesterday when they blew up Dead Water Bridge. That was a tactical victory. But they all still believed then that another Russian surge would be inevitable, that they would capture the town, bring in engineers to make a new bridge, and then push on westwards. Today, they're not so sure.

Now comes the sound of an approaching Russian helicopter.

The aircraft is flying in low from the south, from Mykolaiv, skimming over the cemetery at the top of the hill above Rakove. Then, slowing down, its huge blades thumping the cold air, it comes to land in a field beside a handful of shabby cottages surrounded by Russian armour. One of the Ukrainians near Ghost calls in the coordinates.

Have they seen the stretchers and the Russian soldiers, two by two, straining as they carry their wounded – some wrapped in Svetlana's blankets – over to the field for evacuation? Do they know what they're about to target?

'We treat wolves like wolves,' says one Ukrainian soldier, hardened by eight years fighting the Russians, and remembering countless times when it went the other way, when they were denied the chance to take their wounded off the field.

'And now, our blood is up,' he adds, with a slight shrug.

The first artillery shells land exactly where they're supposed to.

2 3.

For the whole of Thursday, the six of them lie on the floor of the shed in Rakove; Slavik, Roma, Zhenia, Valentyn and the two Russian soldiers accused of sabotage. Not talking much. There's no food, no water and no way to tell the time. The two home guardsmen – acutely conscious of being the most at-risk – tell the others their full names, who to call if they don't make it, and what to say: to tell their families what happened, how they died trying to save the town, and that they had no regrets.

'Are you not married, son?' Slavik asks Zhenia.

'I'm in no hurry,' he replies. A few minutes pass.

'Fucking Rashists,' says Slavik, who never tires of savouring the popular fusion of 'Russian' and 'fascists'.

The thud of artillery continues, some of it close, some in the distance.

And then it's dusk again, and the noises immediately outside the shed grow louder. It feels like something big is being organised. Through a crack in the door, they can see the shadowy outlines of stretchers being moved about and bodies bustling past. Suddenly, they hear the thundering beat of a helicopter. A flying tank, a huge Mi-24 helicopter gunship with space for ten or more men inside comes in low, overhead, from the south-east. It must be landing close by; the rotors are deafening. Minutes pass as the Russians outside load wounded soldiers into the helicopter. Then a shuddering roar, as it starts gathering strength before take-off.

But suddenly there is a mighty explosion, followed by several smaller ones. Inside the shed, they see flashes of bright light, white then yellow. The Ukrainians have landed a direct hit.

A minute later, a Russian soldier, eyes red, face twitching, tears open the shed door and screams.

'Our wounded! They shot them down. They shot the fucking helicopter.'

He swings his AK towards the prisoners, looking for revenge. There's nowhere to move – the shed is a mess of old engine parts, jars, brooms, wood, boxes and tools. Then the man reaches for his knife instead, and Zhenia, once again, believes his moment has come. He can see the soldier trying to decide which method will bring greater satisfaction.

'Let me get them. I'll kill them.'

Suddenly, the soldier is wrestling with a colleague who's grabbed hold of him.

'You're high. Get out of here.' The other soldier is dragging him away from the shed. A few seconds later, the door slams shut.

24.

Down the road in Rakove, Svetlana, Petya and Misha pass another night, even more crowded than the last, in the dank cellar of a friend's house. Svetlana managed to find some pills at home, for her arthritis and her blood pressure, and they have water too now, to share between them all, and warmer clothes. Plus the cat, Sonya, of course, who seems untroubled by the occasional booms from outside, and who lies, purring, on any lap that will have her. Beside Svetlana, Petya sits in silence.

Their younger son lives in Rakove too, in a cottage closer to the river, with cows and pigs in the yard. He is 28 years old, married, with two children – a 5-year-old girl and 9-year-old boy – and he's qualified as a lorry driver but seems to prefer staying closer to home, scraping a living by catching crawfish to sell at the market in Voznesensk. The Russian soldiers came to his house too, yesterday, pointing guns at the kids, giving them 15 minutes to flee. The family escaped to another village further east.

Svetlana rarely sees him these days. She wonders if he's ashamed of his parents. Has their own cottage become too dirty, too dangerous, with Zhulik growling at the gate, and all those bits of salvaged metal waiting to be sold in town? Is their poverty too explicit? The grandchildren almost never come to visit them anymore, never come skipping up the hill to feed their chickens, or to help in the kitchen, making caviar. Well, that's what Svetlana calls it – courgette caviar. Cook the vegetables on the stove for two hours, then add mayonnaise, a head of garlic, tomato paste, lemon juice and chicken stock, then cook it all for another hour. Far better than the stuff in the shops. Her other favourite is Adjika – a Georgian sauce. A great way to preserve a big crop of tomatoes – chopped up or whole, with garlic, horseradish, and chilli pepper. She puts them in jars and stores them until winter.

Svetlana remembers Misha, her older son, on his knees by the gate yesterday morning, with those soldiers around him, threatening to shoot him. He pulled out a bag of documents from his coat, his hands shaking, and pushed them towards the Russians.

'Look, I'm Russian. Like you. Born in Russia. Here's my passport,' said Misha.

On one level, Svetlana was relieved. She was sure the soldier was going to open fire. Her son's reaction probably saved his life. But there was something deeply uncomfortable about it all. They were being forced to take sides; to take the wrong side; to lay claim to a nationality that once seemed almost irrelevant, buried beneath a larger Soviet identity, but which has become, during the course of three decades in Rakove, increasingly foreign, and increasingly repugnant.

On Wednesday, when the soldier poked a gun in her stomach, she made a conscious decision not to mention her own history, not to pin down the details, not to submit to it.

The truth is that Svetlana Martsynkovska, née Korotkova, is Russian. Born to Russian parents on a state farm in a tiny village called Podyom in the Tambov region, south-east of Moscow. When she was fourteen, the family moved to a meat processing plant outside the famous car-manufacturing city of Tolyatti, further east, on the Volga River. She still has a sister and a brother there. It was only much later, after her marriage to Petya, after the Soviet collapse, that they moved to Ukraine. That was back in 1992. The whole country, every region in Ukraine, had just voted for independence from the Soviet Union in a referendum. Even in the Crimea and the Donbas, with their Russian-speaking majorities.

Svetlana remembers Petya's sisters telling them how much easier life would be here. 'Bread and watermelons,' they promised, on the phone. And Petya was happy to move.

But the bureaucracy, and the corruption. It's impossible, a nightmare. They registered in Kyiv, then spent a fortune getting their Russian documents translated into Ukrainian. Then all those trips to Odesa to see a dreadful woman at the passport office. 'A bitch,' Petya declared. They still had their old Soviet passports, and first they were supposed to get them changed to Russian passports. Only after that they could apply for Ukrainian ones. But the cost, and the bribes, and the delays.

In the end, they sold all their cows to help pay for the four of them to get new papers. But they were still Russians, officially. Even Petya, whose old Soviet passport specifically declared that he was Ukrainian. Then they were supposed to update the Russian passports, but the years slipped by, and then there were fines to pay. When Zelenskyy became president, Svetlana remembered that he promised Ukrainian passports for anyone living in Ukraine. But when they went back to check, the woman at the passport office reminded them of the fines they hadn't paid and told them they would have to go and live in Russia for three months and apply from there.

'How can we do that? We're already beggars,' Svetlana told her.

By then the war had started in the east. Travel was impossible. All they wanted was a way to get their Russian pensions, or to get at least some kind of support from the Ukrainian government. Instead, the couple had fallen between two stools. Hence the daily trips to scratch for scraps of metal at the municipal dump. Only Andrii had managed to get his Ukrainian passport, in Mykolaiv. It cost him a fortune, but it was easier for him: he was born here.

25.

The destruction of the Russian helicopter accelerates the invaders' retreat from Voznesensk, and the ebb and flow of battle blurs into something more chaotic, more frantic. The timeline of events blurs too. Everyone remembers everything about Wednesday, almost minute by minute, as the fighting swept through town. But by Thursday evening and beyond, exhaustion gnaws at memory. There's nothing to distinguish one hour from the next as the battle – at first so easy to define by sectors and targets – splinters into a thousand smaller shards of individual drama.

And with that fracturing comes a wildness amongst some of the town's defenders. Weary, outraged fighters catch the intoxicating, adrenalin-fuelling scent of victory and find themselves no longer battling a resolute enemy, but rather chasing desperate men, hunting them like prey.

At around the same time the Russian helicopter is exploding in the field, perhaps a dozen Ukrainian soldiers are moving, on foot, up the main road from town, towards the Shell garage outside Rakove. They're experienced, professional soldiers, a close-knit rapid response team normally focused on counter-sabotage activities. They only arrived late on Tuesday night, to help with the town's defence. Ever since, they've been fighting their way up through Bolgarka, clearing it, together with the 80th Brigade's paratroopers, using RPGs and an NLAW to take out a couple of armoured personnel carriers and a multiple rocket launcher. They haven't lost a single man.

On the way, they capture three Russian soldiers who've been hiding in a cellar. The Russians emerge, shaky hands held high in the air, and are pushed to the ground and searched. Interrogations will come later, but amid the shouts and kicks, one of the Russians tells them that a second assault on Voznesensk was planned for that afternoon.

'We had to abandon it,' says the soldier. Ukrainian artillery strikes have proved too effective. The Russian forces still remaining are all pinned down and looking for ways to retreat.

'That'll do nicely,' one of the Ukrainian soldiers says, a few minutes later, as the group approaches what looks like an abandoned and entirely undamaged Russian tank. Later, they'll drive it into the petrol station, fill it up, and then take it into town as a trophy – one of many. But now, their focus is on clearing and securing more territory.

They count six Russian corpses on the roadside near the station. Some are bandaged. One man looks like he's been run over by a tank. Another is spreadeagled, face down, with his left arm bent awkwardly over his head, as if trying to protect it.

'These fuckers left it all behind, dumped it, for us,' grins a Ukrainian in a black balaclava, looking past the bodies towards an abandoned truck full of mortar shells. Further up the road, another truck-mounted rocket system is lying on its side in the ditch, as if the driver tried and failed to make a hurried U-turn.

And then the soldiers spot the bodies of two local civilians, an elderly man and woman, lying in the dirt. It's obvious from the scale of their injuries that they've both been shot, repeatedly, by a heavy calibre machine gun – the sort that is mounted on the turrets of Russian armoured personnel carriers.

'Like they're on a fucking safari,' one of the Ukrainians mutters angrily, picturing the Russians casually firing on the couple as they sped past.

As they check the woods behind the petrol station, a shot rings out, and then another. The Ukrainians each drop one knee to the ground, then fan out and push forwards. They can see a small group of Russian soldiers ahead. Maybe three of them, crouching behind trees. It is almost immediately clear that they're wounded. For whatever reason, it seems their colleagues must have abandoned them here as they retreated towards Rakove and beyond.

'Come out and surrender,' one of the Ukrainians shouts.

'We will not surrender to Nazis,' comes the reply, followed by another gunshot. But the Russians are out of ammunition, and in no condition to fight.

Exactly what happens next is unclear. Weeks later, on a short break from the frontlines near Mykolaiv, one of the Ukrainians at the scene will talk, with disgust, about the

Russians' lack of honour, the way they left their wounded on the field. He will talk about 300s – Soviet military code for injured soldiers – and 200s – code for dead soldiers. He will mention that the Russians that day were losing blood and were reluctant to surrender. But he will shy away from going into any details.

'We can say that none of those Russians were taken prisoner.'

26.

It's a few hours later on Thursday night, and there are only four prisoners left in Svetlana's shed. The two young Russian soldiers took advantage of the chaos that followed the helicopter crash to slip away. The others are starting to wonder if the attackers might be pulling out altogether, and what that might mean for them.

The door opens and the guard orders Valentyn, Zhenia, Slavik and Roma to come outside, one at a time.

They glance at each other in the gloom; all four of them assume the worst – that they will be taken to the courtyard or the garden and shot. Or maybe they'll use a knife. The men hang back, forcing the Russians to drag them out. They're pushed across the emptying yard. They can see white bandages on the ground and soldiers clambering onto vehicles. Then the men are shoved down the steps into Svetlana's tiny cellar, the one the Nazis once used to store ammunition. It's pitch dark and far colder than the shed. There is a dank, musty smell.

As Slavik, the last of them, tumbles down the bare earthen steps, they change their calculations once more. Surely a grenade will come flying in at any moment. What better way to finish them all off, at arm's length, in such a confined space?

Suddenly, something lands on the earth beside Roma with a soft thud.

27.

It's before dawn on Friday morning and Svetlana sits, weary, dirty, lost in thought, sipping tea in Sasha's kitchen down by the main road in Rakove, not far from the cellar where they've spent the last two nights. Sasha is Slavik's brother, another friend to be found, more often than not, up at the town dump. Misha and Petya are here too. They've come up to get something warm to eat and Sasha has begun frying potatoes in a pan.

What does family mean? What does blood mean? Svetlana wonders.

Three weeks ago, just before the invasion, her brother, Valeri, called her on her mobile. He was in Russia, making a decent living in Tolyatti after leaving the army.

'Why don't you come home? Mother's old apartment is still here. You can stay there. We'll help you with money,' she remembers him saying. Maybe he sensed something, she thought later, something about what was coming.

'I'm getting old. My legs don't work well. Besides, we have a house here now. It's ours. It's something,' Svetlana replied.

'Come on, Sveta. Come back. I'll pay for the transport,' he'd insisted.

She thanked him, but the answer was no. A definite no.

But last week, after the new Russian invasion, their relatives across the border seemed to change their tone, abruptly, overnight. First Petya's sister called, furious, blaming her brother, blaming Ukraine 'for everything', then hanging up in a fury. And after that, Svetlana's brother called again.

'Valera,' she answered. 'Do you know what's happening here? Do you know Russia has attacked us. They're killing, beating, bombing everything, looting . . .'

'This cannot be.' She recognised that sharp, superior, military tone in her younger brother's voice.

'You think your sister would lie about this?' she'd snapped. She knew about Putin's propaganda, the lies spewed on Russian state television on behalf of 'that poisoned dwarf', as Svetlana called him.

'You're making it up. You're fighting with each other, with Nazis. You can't sort yourselves out peacefully, so you blame it on Russians,' said Valeri. So very patronising.

Svetlana's bewilderment was overtaken by her anger.

'Your Putin is talking bullshit,' she said.

'Don't you dare say that!'

'It's true. You are barbarians, murderers. You're killing ordinary people, trying to destroy this nation. Bastards.' Svetlana was shouting.

'You need to sort yourselves out,' said Valeri, coldly, implying that whatever this was, Ukraine had brought it on itself. There was no more to be said.

'Goodbye,' said Svetlana, hanging up before he could.

The memory of that call makes her feel sick. They shared the same parents, still share the same blood, but she cannot imagine ever going back to Russia now. Does she even have relatives there anymore? It seems easier to believe not. Ukraine is her homeland, and that's all there is to it. But still, Svetlana wants to call her sister, Olya, who's living in Tolyatti too. She knows Olya's son has been fighting in Syria as one of the Kremlin's contract soldiers, and she pictures him now, doing the same in Ukraine. She wants to know for sure, she can hear herself asking Olya, 'So, has your boy killed lots of Ukrainians?'

Except that Svetlana doesn't have enough credit on her mobile to speak to Olya. She can receive calls from abroad, but not make them. And somewhere inside, she's still the oldest sister, still a peacemaker.

It seems everyone in Rakove is dealing with similar family ruptures; that everyone has relatives across the border, living in a parallel reality. It's the same on the TV news – Svetlana saw a story about a mother and daughter quarrelling, calling each other Nazis.

But there is some cause for hope. One of Svetlana's neighbours has a son in Novosibirsk, Russia. He had called his mother up to accuse her of lying, telling her there's no war in Ukraine.

'If you don't believe your mother, then you're no longer my son,' she replied.

But a few days later, the son emailed her, apologising, explaining that he'd found the truth on the internet, using a VPN to access independent news.

'You were right mum. I'm sorry I didn't believe you,' he wrote.

28.

Soon after dawn on Friday, an oddly dressed group of men walk up the hill, through Rakove, towards the municipal dump. It's another grey, damp day. Roma, leading the group, can hear birdsong in the stubbled field above Svetlana's cottage. And there, just a few metres from the path, lies the wreckage of the Russian helicopter. Heavy rotors flung far apart. A mess of charred clothing, flesh and twisted metal. The pilot's seat still intact. Smoke rises almost straight into the still, cold, intensely quiet air.

Roma is leading the two guardsmen, Valentyn and Zhenia. They look pitiful, in borrowed boots and old Soviet fur hats with huge ear flaps. Everyone has lost their phones, but Roma has remembered there's a spare in the trailer he uses when he's on night duty at the dump. The soldiers are desperate to tell their families they're still alive.

Zhenia is in a daze, struggling to believe he's made it. How can one go through an ordeal like that with barely a scratch? The Russians have retreated, leaving most of their armour behind. Dozens of wrecked vehicles. Some still on fire, or at least hot to the touch.

A few hours earlier, in Svetlana's cellar, he almost gave up hope. He was braced for a grenade's detonation. But when Roma fumbled in the dark, without thinking, to find what the Russian soldiers had thrown at them, he came across a bottle. Vodka. Slavik found a cigarette lighter, and the men quickly helped tear off the tape still binding Zhenia and Valentyn's hands.

They waited for an hour or so, until the noises outside subsided, and then Roma climbed up the stairs and tried the door. There was a click and it opened. Maybe the Russians had rigged up a grenade on the door. He threw himself back, falling heavily down onto the cellar floor. Silence. Then Zhenia pushed the door again and walked out into courtyard. He could just about make out the rumble of a departing Russian APC. The place was empty and the last of the Russians were gone, evidently in a frantic rush. He peered inside the cottage, his sneakers touching a puddle of congealed blood.

Slavik finished the bottle of vodka all by himself. Then he and the others headed to his brother Sasha's house, on the far side of the main road. He still had food in his kitchen, and soon the kettle was on, and the men sat quietly, sipping tea and eating boiled potatoes, waiting for sunrise. An hour later, the door swung open and Misha, Svetlana and Petya walked in, also in search of food, after another long night in a nearby cellar. Somehow, they had all survived.

29.

After breakfast, the younger men head to the dump, where Roma finds his phone. He, Sasha and the two soldiers take turns calling family, calling friends in town, trying to find out if it is safe to walk into Voznesensk yet, which route to take, and where it's feasible to cross Dead Water River. Roma notices the Russians have syphoned all the petrol from the municipal tractor and he wonders, peering with some interest at the surrounding fields, what will happen to all the new scrap metal now littering the countryside.

The two guardsmen, Zhenia and Valentyn, set off. It's 18 kilometres across town to Valentyn's house. They walk past an abandoned Russian Grad missile launcher, then cut across the fields north of town.

As they're walking home, a tall, 34-year-old man – an appropriately solemn, brooding figure – is heading in the other direction in his small company van. Mykhailo moved to Voznesensk last year, from a city further north, to set up his own funeral company. Now, with the mayor's support, he's decided to begin collecting the bodies, not only of local civilians and the town's civil defence forces, but also of Russian soldiers. They lie scattered around town and across the surrounding hills and woods. He stops the van not far from the dump, shrugs the strap of an AK-47 across a broad shoulder, and pulls a pale blue, transparent plastic body bag out of the back. A Ukrainian soldier who is an explosives expert gets out of the passenger seat to join him. There are concerns that the Russians may have set booby traps on some of their own dead.

No one is sure yet how many Russian soldiers have been killed in the battle. Perhaps one hundred. In the coming days a few will be buried by villagers, hurriedly, in unmarked graves, unknown to the authorities. But Mykhailo feels bound by a sense of professional duty to find as many of their bodies as he can. He's already painted 'Cargo 200' on the side of his van – army shorthand for the dead – in case anyone wonders what he's doing.

He walks over to a soldier's body, lying prone as if sleeping, on a patch of grass already flattened and marked by a tank tread. It strikes him that this work is not just about duty. By doing this, somehow Mykhailo wants to show that his people are better, kinder, more civilised than these brutal invaders, who haven't even bothered to collect all their own dead before retreating.

Once the bodies have been checked for explosives, he searches their clothes. Most are carrying nothing, or have already been searched by others, but he pockets a notebook, a few icons, and some Russian military passports to hand over to Ukrainian army intelligence. 'Victor Nikolaivitch Yegorov, tank operator, certificate 1586' – a photo of a pale young face staring out from behind a long fringe. 'Pankiv Vi . . .' – the rest of the name too charred to read. And so on.

Once his van is full, Mykhailo drives back across town, to the railway station. There's a long cargo wagon on a siding, and he and some other men haul the bodies inside, lying them shoulder to shoulder in a neat row across the cold, ridged, metal floor. He tells himself that he's helping local people, removing evidence of the invaders from sight and saving the community from further trauma.

But another, angrier part of him imagines loading these bodies into a plane, flying to Moscow, and circling over the city, dropping the corpses on the streets below. He wants ordinary people there to be shaken awake, to realise what their government is really doing here with its 'special military operation'.

30.

While the funeral director is scouring the fields for bodies, a young Russian soldier knocks on the gate of a cottage in a small settlement called Stepove, a cluster of about thirty cottages to the north of Rakove. Two elderly women open the gate warily. There are still a few loud booms nearby. Ukrainian artillery and mortars are pounding Russian troops as they haphazardly retreat.

'Please, I'm looking for Ukrainian soldiers. I want to surrender,' says the soldier, barely out of his teens, looking cold and scared.

At this point, Ghost and his team have already taken two other prisoners: a 21-year-old and a 31-year-old, who surprised them by simply walking out of a house in the same settlement with their hands in the air. As they escorted the soldiers, on foot, back into town, Ghost talked to them. The younger man said he was Russian, and then kept quiet. But the older one admitted he was Crimean, that he'd grown up there, went to school, and lived there as a Ukrainian, even travelling to Kyiv.

'So, a proper traitor,' Ghost spat out.

'It's not my war,' the soldier replied.

There was something odd about this older man. He said his name was Alexei Abramov, and that he was just a contractor, a gun for hire on his second job with the Russian military. But it's only now, when Ghost and his unit return to the settlement, that things start making sense. They run into the elderly women with their young Russian captive.

Ghost quickly notices this new prisoner's clothes. His uniform looks too smart, like something an officer might wear. The young man claims he bought his jacket in Crimea, but Russian soldiers don't have the right to wear what they like. A little later, after they've dropped their new prisoner with the 80th Brigade, at the headquarters below the bookshop, Ghost comes across a stash of documents in an abandoned Russian APC that's sitting in someone's back garden. Inside it, there are lists of names and stacks of military passports, and on one of the lists Ghost spots the name 'Abramov', with the job title: 'military intelligence'.

He calls Formosa to share his theory about Abramov. The senior soldier, a trained spy, must have lost contact with the rest of the column, realised he'd been abandoned and then ordered one of his young subordinates to swap clothes with him. Then he must have told him to go and lie low somewhere in the settlement before surrendering. Meanwhile Abramov – pretending to be a lowly contract soldier of little value to the Ukrainians – would hand himself over, hoping he would be treated more leniently and perhaps quickly traded for a Ukrainian prisoner of war.

Formosa is inclined to believe it. His team has already begun interrogating nearly a dozen other Russian prisoners at his headquarters in the town centre, and, so far, every single one of them has come up with an unlikely story about their low military status. One mortar unit claimed they were all cooks and doctors. A couple of other soldiers insisted they didn't actually fire any weapons – they were just doing logistics.

'So, who is actually fighting against us then,' Formosa asks one group of prisoners, his voice thick with sarcasm.

No one says anything.

31.

A pale body is lying on a hospital stretcher. You can see tufts of black chest hair and, just above them, a delicate metal necklace. The torso appears unharmed – it's the body of a young, fit man. There are blue tiled walls behind him and two medical canisters on a small white table, beside the man's head. And it is the head that demands attention. It looks like it belongs to another body entirely. The neck is pale white, but from just under the chin, the skin becomes a dark blackish-green. It's as if he's wearing stage paint. His eyes are closed and his eyelids, eyebrows, ears and a scrap of cropped hair high on his head look as they've been scorched black.

And then the soldier's mouth twitches. His lips are grotesque, swollen, glistening – curdled pink and yellow, like two sausages sweating on a barbeque. And now the man is trying to answer a question.

'Once again, what was your job?'

'Evacuation of the wounded.' The words come out in a gargled whisper, exhaled, painfully. His eyelids flicker but don't open and it becomes clear that they're sealed together, welded shut by the heat that must have seared his whole head.

'Evacuation of the wounded from where?'

The interrogator's voice is clipped.

'From Voznesensk . . . there was . . . a site.' The words seep out of the wounded soldier – each more painful than the last.

'Where was the site?'

The soldier talks about 'the north', then changes his mind and whispers 'south'.

'To the south of Voznesensk there was a site from which you evacuated the wounded?'

'Yes.'

'Where were you supposed to take them?'

'To Kherson,' he answers.

'Where in Kherson?'

'A kind of hospital.'

The questions are insistent, but curiously neutral. There's no direct threat of violence. But there's also no hint of sympathy. The questioner's indifference is exaggerated, he sounds like a bored teacher with a disappointing student. Above all, it is a display of power and, along with it, a glimpse into the bureaucracy of war; the gathering of information, the processing of a prisoner, the accumulation of evidence.

But maybe there's more to it than that. Because the man asking the questions is no mere junior bureaucrat making his way round the wards of Voznesensk hospital. General Dmytro Marchenko – call sign 'Marcello' – is the commander of

Ukraine's forces in nearby Mykolaiv, which is still under intense Russian attack from three sides.

A portly man with a shaved head and small blue eyes, General Marchenko's gruff optimism has turned him into a totemic figure in southern Ukraine as he strides around Mykolaiv's frontlines and field hospitals, offering withering assessments of Russia's abilities, and morale-boosting quips about a Ukrainian victory. His reputation is only outshone by one man, the regional governor, Vitalii Kim, known for his nonchalant, uplifting video messages.

'Good evening. We're from Ukraine.'

It is one of Kim's catchphrases. He half grins, barely tries to hide a tired yawn, then lists the latest daytime or overnight damage, the residential neighbourhoods hit by Russian rockets.

'Good night . . . I wish everyone a boring night.'

It feels as if Kim and Marchenko are the older brothers of the mayor and Formosa, down the road in tiny Voznesensk; and the connection is real. Over the past couple of days, Ukrainian troops have successfully pushed the enemy from Mykolaiv's outskirts, halting, for now, the Kremlin's attempt to push west from Kherson and march on to Odesa. But General Marchenko's victories led, directly, to Voznesensk's challenges, as the Russians became increasingly desperate to find a different crossing point over the Southern Buh River.

Which helps to explain why a badly injured Russian soldier is now being interrogated by the general himself. The soldier is a young helicopter pilot. He was the one who landed the huge Mi-24 in the field behind Svetlana's cottage on Thursday evening to collect wounded soldiers, seconds before the chopper was incinerated by Ukrainian artillery. Somehow, he must have escaped from the wreckage. He's ended up at a hospital in Mykolaiv, but it's not clear exactly how, given that the road from Voznesensk is still extremely dangerous.

'Understood.' General Marchenko is nearly done with his interrogation and his voice briefly sounds more casual, like someone who has merely been asking for directions. But then it changes again.

'Did you see your dead comrades?' the general asks.

It's not really a question – it's a rebuke, a gesture of contempt, of disgust. A woman's voice cuts in. The doctors need to attend to their patient. The pilot's eyes remain firmly shut, but slowly, he shakes his head.

'I doubt they survived,' the pilot whispers.

'Understood,' says the general, and this time you can hear the disdain, sharp and clear, bouncing off the hospital walls, as he turns on his heels and marches away to the next meeting, the next frontline, the next stage of this murderous absurdity.

32.

In the coming weeks, locals will place a new statue of the Virgin Mary beside the ruins of Dead Water Bridge. But not yet. The Russians have gone, but for now there is no celebration. No bell tolls. There's not even a collective roar like there was in the mayor's office, on Tuesday 1st March, when the 80th destroyed a section of the approaching Russian column. It all feels too raw and unfinished for festivities.

Andrii's soon-to-be-ex-wife and daughter are still trapped, and under fire, in a village near Kherson. The mayor's uncle has been taken prisoner by Russian troops while fighting in the Donbas. And Formosa is pursing what's left of Russia's 126th Brigade, first pushing it out of artillery range of the town, then further back, past the next small towns to the east and on towards the Dnipro River. At some point it looks like the Russians are being ordered to try another route to get around Voznesensk, but the 80th quickly cut them off.

In town, Anna Ahapytova, has been searching for her son, 21-year-old Serhii. Hours before he was killed by the tank shell outside the fireman's cottage, she begged him not to get involved.

'Leave it to the soldiers,' she said, as he ran out the door to join his friends.

Anna works four or five nights a week at the town's hospital. She's not a qualified nurse, but she keeps an eye on the patients, bringing them water, changing their beds and chatting. For the past six years she has worked there most evenings, a brisk 20-minute walk, just past the railway station.

She usually heads home, early in the morning, and dozes for a couple of hours before starting her other job, at a stall in the market. She's never needed much sleep – three or four hours is plenty – and somehow the routine suits her. She's a fast talker, a sturdy woman with gingery hair, and a habit of clutching her neck when she becomes emotional.

Eleven bodies were brought into the hospital morgue that first night of the battle, including one Russian. Before long, Anna got word that her son was missing. But no one seemed able to say more. His friends weren't answering their phones. The doctors were all too busy to help. When she finally went down to the morgue, she saw a severed leg beside the other bodies and immediately wondered if it belonged to Serhii.

It's not until Friday morning that Anna reaches 53 Tamaschyshyna Street and is left in no doubt. She's been looking all over town for him, ignoring the explosions, failing to get an answer at the police station, before someone tells her the address and urges her to hurry – the dogs are starting to pick at the remains. Something strange comes over her.

Now she walks past the gate, which stands wide open, buckled by the blast and riddled with shrapnel, and surveys the dusty carnage in front of her. Rather than recoiling, she feels an urgent, visceral need to collect every piece of her son, to put Serhii back together. And so, she takes a bag, kneels on the ground, and begins picking up lumps of flesh.

It takes hours. She even scrapes bits of him off the gate, murmuring to herself.

'This is him. That's his flesh.'

And only then, after she's filled the bag and has begun walking back across town to the morgue, does she begin to sob.

A few days later, someone at the town hall brushes off Anna's request that her son be recognised as a volunteer fighter rather than just some civilian who got unlucky.

'What do you want? This is war,' they say to her.

But she's persistent. She's found the security video footage of the explosion and keeps asking for help. In the end the mayor's office relents, giving her a modest contribution to the funeral, and she has a small gathering at her home. Nothing fancy – there's no power or water in her building – just a few sweets and some drinks. The closed coffin lies in the sitting room.

That afternoon, a hundred people turn up for the burial in a crowded corner of the cemetery, near the road where Serhii used to sell watermelons as a child.

'Not the best spot, hidden away here. And just a simple wooden cross,' Anna reflects.

Still, it's a good turnout, with lots of flowers placed on top of a mound of freshly dug earth. The mayor comes along and says a few words. He calls her boy a hero.

3 3 .

It's a clear, sweltering afternoon in early August 2022, and Svetlana walks stiffly through her vegetable garden. She's dressed in a bright green short-sleeved top and brown leggings, her silver-grey hair is tied up in a bun, and one sun-bronzed arm clutches a stick. She tuts quietly under her breath. The grass, flattened by Russian tank tracks five months ago, is knee high once more but the rain has been scarce this summer, the soil on this exposed hillside is not good, and the tomatoes and squashes have produced precious little for Svetlana's jars.

'Oy,' she sighs deeply. Then she grabs hold of my arm and steers us back towards her cottage.

It's the end of my third month reporting from Ukraine's frontlines for BBC News. I've been staying down the road, in Mykolaiv, but the Russian bombardment of the city centre is intensifying. Apartment blocks are being turned to rubble every day. Two nights ago, a nearby school building was hit by a cruise missile. Yesterday morning we walked outside, after a third sleepless night, to see a huge, unexploded missile sticking into the tarmac a few yards away, like a cartoonish bad joke. So, we've decided to decamp to Voznesensk.

The town has only suffered one significant bombardment in recent days – an attempt, last night, to hit a military storage depot full of rusting decommissioned tanks on the far side of town. The Kremlin quickly claimed it had destroyed vast amounts of valuable weaponry, but it's not true. Most – if not all – the rockets landed short. One of them crashed through the roof of a stone mason's empty cottage in a small village north of here.

'Ours,' says Svetlana, suddenly, pointing up at the blue sky, where a lone Ukrainian fighter jet races towards Russian lines far overhead.

It's an unremarkable thing to say, but her use of that pronoun feels loaded now with a sense of both pride and loss. I immediately think of how the same word – *nashi* in Russian – was claimed by Putin as the name of a thuggish, pro-Kremlin youth group.

On my way up the hill, an hour ago, I spotted Svetlana's neighbour, Mikhail, rather gloriously standing in leather boots and a pair of faded grey underpants, scything the field beside his cottage. Mikhail and his wife remain an isolated couple in Rakove, and the focus of pointed gossip.

'Did you speak to him? I hope you didn't mention my name,' says Svetlana, later.

In fact, I did stop to chat with Mikhail, who put down his scythe and walked over to the fence on stiff, bowed legs. His muscles and sinews stood out, precise and anatomical, on his scrawny arms and chest.

'Good to meet you. It gets lonely here,' he said, as we shook hands. 'What are people telling you? That my wife and I are collaborators?'

I nodded, feeling a little awkward. There's been lots of talk about them, and about another unnamed woman, who was supposedly seen guiding the Russians through Bolgarka in a white car. So far, no charges have been pressed.

'Well, I won't say I'm against Russia. I don't have that feeling. I can't be too hard on them since I've still got brothers, a sister, grandchildren living there,' he said, and went on to describe how he'd encountered the first Russian soldiers, back in March, after their convoy came under fire.

'They behaved decently. Young lads from Crimea. Normal guys doing their business. They came up here and built their trenches. I looked on them like my own grandsons.'

He doesn't say if he and his wife fed them or helped them in any other way, and I don't feel comfortable asking. He does say that when a Russian officer took their phones, he returned them straight away in a rare display of trust.

And then Mikhail starts telling his own story, of how Russia's Empress, Catherine the Great, had sent his ancestors here, to populate the half-empty lands around the Black Sea. How he'd been born in Soviet Ukraine, studied engineering at a college near the Caspian Sea, had fought in Afghanistan, then moved to Leningrad, then to Karelia in Russia's far north.

'When there was a Soviet Union, we were all brothers and sisters. In my unit in Afghanistan, we had fifteen nationalities. We shared one spoon, ate off one plate. We were a family. And now,' he pauses, waving one hand to indicate the other cottages on the sun-baked hillside around him. 'Now all this. It doesn't sit well with me.'

What makes one family pick one path, while a few hundred yards up the same hill their neighbours take another? Mikhail's story reminds me so much of Svetlana's. The same Soviet nostalgia, the same grumbling about pensions. Mikhail has also had to sell all his cattle, and cars too, and has ended up on the outskirts of Rakove, stranded and poor, baffled by a fast-changing world. He feels Russian, and Soviet, and Ukrainian. A Venn diagram of overlapping loyalties. Why should he be forced to take sides?

But Svetlana has made her choice – quickly, resolutely – and it seems to me that in taking refuge in ambiguity, Mikhail has made another.

The door to Svetlana's cottage, no longer employed as a make-shift stretcher, is back on its hinges. The courtyard is now shaded by deep green vines and is more cluttered with bits of scavenged metal and timber and roof tiles than ever. Fenced off in a corner are two turkeys, being fattened up to sell at Christmas. Zhulik the dog looks like he'd make short work of them both if he could pull off his chain. The surrounding fields have long since been cleared of abandoned Russian armour, but there are still a few empty dark-green plastic ration packs in the undergrowth.

Svetlana leaves her courgette caviar stewing in the kitchen and reaches under her bed to find the tattered plastic bag containing her photograph albums. She's already crying before she opens the first book and turns the pages to stop at a black-and-white photo of her brother's wedding from the 1980s – all bowties, sashes, bouquets and smiles. Svetlana goes quiet. The siblings have still not spoken since the early days of the war.

'Such is our life,' she says, closing the album with a sudden snap.

One week from now, a Russian missile will hit an apartment block in the centre of Voznesensk, injuring eighteen people, including three children. But today the town feels relaxed. A young girl is rollerblading down October Revolution Street, an infant in a pram clutches yellow balloons. A farmer, pulling a cart piled high with straw, drives past four bearded young men smoking shisha pipes opposite the park. There are watermelons on sale, and two women, cycling past each other in summer dresses near the railway station, say 'beep-beep' to each other, then laugh.

The mayor, Yevhenii, is back in his office. He looks several years older than he did in March. But he talks with the same furious energy, rattling off plans to build bomb shelters in every school and to prepare for an influx of thousands more displaced families. The fish tank in the conference room hums in the background. Someone must have remembered to come back to the building during those chaotic early weeks to feed the fish.

'We've become a friendlier town in these past months, more relaxed. We've buried our little local grievances. People call us all the time and ask, "How can we help? What do you need?"' Yevhenii says earnestly.

Two dozen local people have gathered in the cellar which once acted as the mayor's temporary office. They are here to listen to a lecture about how to use plastic sheets in their gardens to increase their vegetable crop yields. As I sit in the back row, I get the sense of a community daring to imagine a future beyond tomorrow once again.

Just along the street, Dead Water Bridge still lies in ruins. But a few hundred yards downstream, a new temporary road crossing has been built out of sewage pipes and rubble. The pipes have been mined with explosive charges, just in case the Russians return, and the local defence forces are primed to blow the crossing up at any moment.

Ghost and most of his colleagues have been fighting near Kherson. In a few months the city will be recaptured by Ukrainian forces. Right now, he's home on leave, but still 'combat ready,' with his AK-47 and other supplies in the back seat of his Renault.

Anna, whose son Serhii was killed by a tank shell near Dead Water Bridge, visits his grave every evening on her way to the local hospital where she continues to work. The wards are full of casualties from Mykolaiv and the nearby frontlines. Forty-five people were brought in last night alone.

Zhenia and Valentyn, the volunteer soldiers who ended up as prisoners in Svetlana's shed, are both struggling to find work, but ready to be called up again to defend their town. Two days after Valentyn got home, his adopted cat gave birth to two kittens. One of them, plump and with black and white markings, sits contentedly on his narrow bed.

'I call him Boris. After your prime minister. And he bites,' he adds with a smile, holding up a freshly bandaged thumb. It's taken Valentyn months to find some sense of calm, in his head and heart.

Igor Rudenko, the 126th Brigade officer captured by Ukrainians, is in prison. Although he was serving in the Russian army, prosecutors argue that since he's a Ukrainian himself, he can't be included in any prisoner swaps. Instead, he has had to answer to Ukraine's own criminal justice system. He was charged with desertion and treason, and after a two-day trial in Kyiv, in April 2022, he was found guilty on both counts and sentenced to fifteen years in prison.

We may never know, for sure, what impact the brief, decisive battle in Voznesensk had on the larger course of the war in Ukraine. If the town's defenders had chosen not to make a stand – had left it to another town, another bridge, another community to risk everything. Perhaps Russian troops would have pushed on and seized the great port city of Odesa. Perhaps the Kremlin would have been able to make an amphibious landing further along the coast. Perhaps Mykolaiv would have fallen too, along with the whole of southern Ukraine. Perhaps the war might then have taken a very different turn.

* * *

It is later that same hot August afternoon and we've driven from Rakove, across the mayor's new makeshift bridge, wandered around town, and then turned south. We weave our way past rows of neat cottages, to the eastern bank of the broad, brown Southern Buh River.

'Miami beach,' says Andrii, the deputy mayor, proudly pointing to a long stripe of yellow sand that has been newly added to the riverbank from a local quarry. There are big new wooden beach loungers and a new volleyball court. Perhaps a dozen families are here, picnicking, splashing in the slow-flowing water or sunbathing on their towels. Or, following that curious Soviet tradition that older people sometimes still prefer, standing up to sunbathe. Somewhere to the south, out of sight, another Ukrainian warplane roars past, but no one says anything. And although no one articulates it, we can all feel it, a group of us standing at the top of the unfinished concrete steps that lead down to the beach, listening to the children shouting and a radio playing music.

This is what defiance feels like.

Afterword

I first came to Voznesensk in March 2022, soon after the battle, on a winding, pot-holed, axle-snapping country road, with the boom of artillery audible in the distance. We made a television report about what had happened, which you should be able to find easily enough on YouTube, if you're interested in seeing Svetlana and her cottage, and the mayor, and a video of Alexander Moskaliuk shouting, 'You little beauties!' as Ukrainian soldiers fired towards the Russian convoy when it approached Dead Water Bridge.

I used to live in the former Soviet Union. I arrived in Moscow as a would-be foreign correspondent in 1991, weeks before the USSR quietly collapsed. I travelled widely – including many trips to Ukraine – and only left, almost a decade later, in 2000, just as a glum former KGB officer with a strutting, swaggering gait was taking control in the Kremlin.

I speak Russian – imperfectly – and have a deep love of the language and culture. Coming to the end of this book, after a whole year of war in Ukraine, I've often recalled the end lines of Chekhov's famous short story, 'The Lady with the Dog' – a story largely set in the Crimea and Moscow.

'*And it was clear to both of them that they still had a long, long road before them, and that the most complicated and difficult part of it was only just beginning.*'

As the war has dragged on, I've became increasingly aware of the toll it is taking, not only in lives and in the savage, spiteful destruction of so many homes and infrastructure, but also on the minds and mental health of some Ukrainians who – it seems to me – are becoming haunted by the notion that this conflict may never end, and by the fear that Russia's capacity to absorb suffering and its unflinching willingness to continue inflicting it, will eventually enable it to grind out some kind of victory.

You rarely hear such fears expressed 'on the record', and the confidence and optimism of so many Ukrainians remains genuine, inspiring and, I believe, well placed. My aim with this short book is to shine a small light on one rousing and revealing episode, but I am conscious of the fact that the outcome of the wider war remains profoundly uncertain.

When Ukrainian friends talk about their anxieties, and the deep weariness that comes with being forced to live a life of such constant and unending insecurity, I think of a meeting I had one night, recently, in the Donbas, with a punk rock singer who is also a medical doctor and was busy patching up the wounded as they flooded into an army field hospital from the town of Bakhmut. His coping mechanism, he explained during a break, with a broad smile and another sip of coffee, was to take a step back from the world around him, and to try to live in an imagined reality – in the cheerful world he pictures after Ukraine's victory.

'This is how we live through the war. By living in our dreams,' he told me.

This book is based on dozens of interviews with those involved, and on videos they've shared with me. I've also used material from other sources and have sought to pull it all together in a novelistic style that, at times, involves recreating scenes from hazy and imperfect memories. I hope the results fairly reflect what happened in Voznesensk during those few, frenzied days. Any errors in fact or judgement are my own.

Afterword to the Paperback Edition

Part Two

It is now two years since the battle of Voznesensk and one year since I finished writing this book. An update of sorts seems appropriate.

The frontline in south-eastern Ukraine has now retreated well over an hour's drive to the east of Svetlana's cottage, and fresh hints of normality have returned to the neighbourhood, and, indeed, to the region.

On quieter days when clouds muffle the roar of passing fighter jets and people are distracted, for instance, by the rush to bring in crops from the vast, undulating fields around town, it is even possible to imagine that the war has ended.

In recent months a scheme to put electric scooters on the streets of Voznesensk has been unveiled. The local sushi restaurant has a new "Fantasy" deal for larger groups of diners. The police have launched a new campaign against online fraudsters and are still investigating a fatal car crash near the centre of town. Several men from Voznesensk won prizes at a wrestling tournament in a nearby town, and a team of eight- and nine-year-old children returned from Belgium, having won second place in a European karate competition.

These are the ups and downs of ordinary life, and a glimpse of a world that might have prevailed, had Russia come to terms with its tortured history, and left its neighbours undisturbed.

But the sense of normality only superficial. Most days, and indeed most hours here, it remains hard for anyone to forget the invasion. The war, the deaths, the low-level throb of existential dread, the sheer madness of it all, still claw at the throat. You can see it in the big, solemn crowds that come out – here and in every town and village across Ukraine – for the funerals.

'We ask the community to form a lively corridor to honour our Hero!' says one invitation after another.

And sure enough, people turn out in their hundreds to throw flowers in the path of each slow procession, as the coffin is carried from the family home, through town, to the big cemetery near the hospital, or across the bridge – now under reconstruction – to another cemetery in the eastern suburbs.

Ivan was killed on the Luhansk frontlines. Bohdan died during a mission in Donetsk. Pavlo, killed during fierce fighting to defend northern Ukraine. Mykola died in the line of duty on the southern front, near Zaporizhzhia. And on it goes. The authorities are still keeping the official death toll secret, but there is a clear sense that every corner of Ukraine is paying a steep price in blood to continue this war with Russia.

'We bow our heads in mourning. We share your grief. Heroes don't die, they stay in our hearts. Let us forever remember our glorious defenders of Ukraine!'

'This hellish war continues to take away those closest to us.'

A 'Path of Remembrance' has recently been built outside the administration building in the centre of Voznesensk, with photographs and details of those locals who've died in the line of duty. Schools are doing something similar, with special bushes planted to honour the dead. And every local event, every municipal budget line, every charitable organisation, every school trip, is now coloured by the war and focused either on helping to secure victory or on coping with the impact of Russia's offensive and of a conflict that has lasted far too long.

Widows run online petitions for their dead husbands to be awarded posthumous 'hero' status by the state.

'He gave his life for our freedom. He died as a result of mortar fire by the enemy. He is forever 32 years old,' writes one woman.

School children recently organised an online photography competition with the theme of 'togetherness' to support displaced families now living in Voznesensk. Five veterans with prosthetic legs went on a sponsored walk in the nearby hills to raise money for other wounded soldiers. School number eight has raised enough money to buy a motorboat for a rifle company in the 123rd Brigade as part of a 'funds, not flowers' campaign for the armed forces.

But that sense of civic purpose, of a community entirely dedicated to supporting the war effort, is only one part of an increasingly fractious equation. One of the many ways in which Ukrainians tend to differentiate themselves from Russians is by pointing to their culture of feisty scepticism towards authority, and their reluctance, throughout history, to tolerate any kind of unelected leader or Tzar. As the conflict has dragged on and the sacrifices have grown, public tolerance for official corruption or ineptitude – deeply engrained features of post-Soviet life – has been replaced by a new and very public spirit of rage and determination.

'Our government steals and steals and pisses in our faces,' a local man fumes on Voznesensk's municipal Facebook page.

'People are tired of the fact that they fight alone, die, become disabled,' he continues, reacting to news reports that more than twenty thousand pounds allegedly went missing in the early days of the war due to corruption in the mayor's office. Others amplify that indignation in public meetings with the town's administration. The police later confirm that a 30-year-old woman and another senior figure in the municipality – someone who features in this book – are under investigation for bypassing standard procurement processes and purchasing drones, night-vision goggles, camouflage, and other equipment at inflated prices.

Some will argue that this is proof that the Ukrainian state, however impressively it may have rallied to fight off the Russian invasion, is still a fundamentally rotten, oligarch-ridden kleptocracy that is using the conflict as a cover and an excuse for further looting. But there is another, more encouraging interpretation of what's happening in places like Voznesensk.

'Let me tell you how it happened,' the town's young mayor says to me, soon after news of several arrests comes out.

As he, and others, put it, Ukraine is remaking itself. It's a process that began long before this latest Russian invasion, but which the current phase of the war has accelerated. The institutions of state are being reformed. The police, the prosecution services, are being cleaned up. And a young, tech-savvy generation of new leaders is shaking up local government. Which is why, in the frantic, chaotic hours and days after the Russian invasion, Voznesensk's municipal office bypassed formal government structures in order to buy military equipment for its local defenders with greater speed and efficiency. 'The lives of our soldiers depended on it,' says the mayor. And it's also why a vigorous prosecution service is now investigating those purchases, as you'd expect in any law-abiding state.

Convinced? The truth will emerge in time.

For now, Ukraine has a war to win and, as the casualties mount, a growing preoccupation with time and with the speed of that victory. Indeed, in some ways it feels as if time itself has been warped by the war. First came those terror-torn days, with hours blurred into seconds. Then dull, anxious weeks, curdled into months. And now time – wartime – is held hostage by an unknowable future, and by the cloying uncertainty that now infects every waking moment. When will a husband return from the frontlines? Will the war still be going when a son turns eighteen? When should a family return from abroad? When will it all be over?

Meanwhile, Svetlana has been grappling with yet another winter. She's lost a little weight in recent months and feels the cold more than usual as she pads around the courtyard, still without her pension, a scarf wrapped tightly around her head. Her men have been busy, on and off, hunting for more scraps of metal and doing other odd jobs in the neighbourhood. They recently got hold of two big bags of onions, in less than perfect condition, which should, nonetheless, last the three of them for a few months.

Across the road, their pro-Russian neighbours are still keeping themselves to themselves. Mikhail's leg is no better. It seems that their son was recently given a nine-year prison sentence for helping Russian troops and killing two civilians in Voznesensk.

Svetlana's Russian relatives haven't been back in touch. And perhaps that's for the best. But she's heard that a nephew, who joined the Wagner Group, was injured in combat.

And, so, on a quiet hillside above Rakove village, life stumbles on. Svetlana is finding it a little harder to walk far these days. But she can do her daily chores and feed the chickens that squawk every time one of the dogs gets close to the makeshift fence. The outhouse is still in ruins, and the weather has been too dry for a decent harvest of potatoes. But the cucumbers and raspberries came through just fine. Svetlana has pickled some courgettes too. And best of all is the progress shown by her pear tree, once split open and broken by a Russian tank, but now a mess of eager new branches, like a child's hasty scribble. And already one small crop of budding fruits.

Acknowledgements

I didn't steal these stories. But I did, sometimes, snatch at them, in the middle of an all-consuming war, from people who had far too little time on their hands and far more urgent business to preoccupy them.

On my fourth trip to Ukraine, in the grey, icy weeks of January 2023, I finally caught up, in person, with Formosa, who, by then, was no longer commander of the 80th Brigade. I met him close to the frontlines elsewhere in eastern Ukraine, in a wooded area, and amid conditions of great secrecy, with the distant thump of artillery punctuating our conversation. He was in a rush, as always, and was starting a new and important job, with a new military offensive to plan. But he told me he also recognised something special in the story of Voznesensk – and that he believed that one small, decisive and improbable victory there had almost certainly saved Ukraine from a larger encirclement, and – most likely – from the prospect of defeat. And so, he spoke, in his hushed, hurried voice, about his strategy for the town, the logistics of the battle, the struggle to destroy Dead Water Bridge and his unusual call sign. And then he answered the many follow-up questions I sent to him via WhatsApp. I later heard that Voznesensk has now named a street after the 80th Brigade.

Svetlana Martsynkovska is the soul of this book – if it can lay claim to one. I certainly would not have considered writing it without her support and cooperation. She has a phenomenal, enthusiastic capacity to recall conversations and details and brief exchanges, and to repeat them as if they're happening again in front of her. From our very first meeting, on a darkening afternoon in March 2022, she seemed to take me under her wing, eager to show me every scratch and bloodstain in her cottage, and equally willing to share her own remarkable history, and the minutiae and struggles of her family life.

Like Svetlana, the mayor, Yevhenii Velychko, his deputy, Andrii Zhukov, Spartak, Ghost, Anna Ahapytova, Serhii Potushynskyi, Roma, Oleg, the home guards Valentyn and Zhenia, Alexander Moskaliuk, the town's museum director, soldiers, volunteers, and many others in Voznesensk were generous with their time and their stories. Even during the dead of winter, when the power was frequently off, or preciously rationed, they put up with my frequent requests – on WhatsApp, Zoom, Signal, Viber and more – for extra details and new insights. I am deeply grateful to them all, and to everyone who appears in this book, for their time and patience.

I want to mention the remarkable journalists – many of them old friends and colleagues – who've been covering this conflict. There is something about working in a warzone that often brings out the best in people – and that is true of the journalist's trade too. We depend on our traditional rivals for advice that could save lives. We share information about unsafe roads, about unpredictable towns and checkpoints, and routinely celebrate the work and the scoops and the courage of our competitors. In that spirit, I want to offer a special thanks to Yaroslav Trofimov, an extraordinarily brave correspondent with *The Wall Street Journal*, who first alerted me to the details of the battle of Voznesensk with a powerful report from the town.

Another common feature of working in warzones is that you get to meet and work alongside a far wider group of people than you tend to do in less chaotic and less stressful situations. Andrii Pechatkin is a musician and member of the 'deviant black metal' band, White Ward. We met, almost by chance, in Odesa in early March 2022, and he's become a good friend, as well as being a superb translator and fixer. Artyom Belov – a formidably well-connected, passionate and fearless former soldier, policeman and cameraman – has guided me and my colleagues around countless frontlines and far beyond. Sasha Oseredchuk, a retired Donbas miner, along with his son and son-in-law, have driven our team through the mud, dust and snow. Thanks to Anton Kurkov in Kyiv and to Bogdan Kolesnyk. Volodymyr Lozhko was incredibly helpful on the correct spelling and transliteration of Ukrainian names. Thanks to Serhii Zhadan for allowing me to quote from his poem, 'Rhinoceros'. I've used the translation from *Words for War: New Poems from Ukraine* www.wordsforwar.

com/rhinoceros. From the BBC, Hanna Tsyba, Anna Chornous and Mariana Matveichuk have been generous with their expertise. Joe Phua remains the kindest, most gifted cameraman and comrade. Melanie Marshall, Thanya Doksone, Naomi Scherbel-Ball and Ed Habershon are wonderful producers and friends. Simon Roughton, Kevin Sissons, Jake Jacobs, Steve Byrne, Zak Dunnings and Terry Carter have watched our backs diligently. Further afield, I'm grateful to Paul Danahar, Alan Quartly and Vlad Hernandez for their support.

I owe particular thanks to my magical, tireless agent, Rebecca Carter, for steering this book to a publisher. Sarah Braybrooke is that publisher, and what a brilliantly perceptive, thoughtful, and talented editor and guide she has been, along with her great team at Ithaka and Bonnier, and freelance copy-editor Susan Pegg. Thanks also to Jonathan Kinnersley at The Agency.

Lastly, my family. My three sons are setting off on their own paths now, but they continue to be a source of deep joy, pride and laughter. Our large dog, Albert, requires a small mention for his traditional role, sitting – occasionally patiently – beneath my desk during much of the writing process. But it is my wife, Jenny, to whom I owe the most – for her generous support, and for her love, insight and humour, which continue to make everything worthwhile.

A Note on Spelling

Many Ukrainians – now more than ever – are anxious to rescue their language from Russia's long shadow. That applies to the way words are transliterated into the Latin alphabet. The most well-known instance of this is Ukraine's capital, once known internationally as 'Kiev' – a transliteration of the Russian Cyrillic spelling of the city – but now changed to 'Kyiv' to better reflect its Ukrainian spelling and pronunciation.

I have sought, in this book, to use Ukrainian transliterations of names and places, except where individuals have made clear their own preferences. This is a delicate, and sometimes complicated, issue with inevitable political implications. Although there are now clear official rules, there are, hardly surprisingly, still some discrepancies.

Mango Publishing, established in 2014, publishes an eclectic list of books by diverse authors—both new and established voices—on topics ranging from business, personal growth, women's empowerment, LGBTQ studies, health, and spirituality to history, popular culture, time management, decluttering, lifestyle, mental wellness, aging, and sustainable living. We were named 2019 and 2020's #1 fastest growing independent publisher by Publishers Weekly. Our success is driven by our main goal, which is to publish high-quality books that will entertain readers as well as make a positive difference in their lives.

Our readers are our most important resource; we value your input, suggestions, and ideas. We'd love to hear from you—after all, we are publishing books for you! Please stay in touch with us and follow us at:

Facebook: Mango Publishing

Twitter: @MangoPublishing

Instagram: @MangoPublishing

LinkedIn: Mango Publishing

Pinterest: Mango Publishing

Newsletter: mangopublishinggroup.com/newsletter

Join us on Mango's journey to reinvent publishing, one book at a time.